MW00997157

Picture A Garden

Written and Illustrated by

Linda Hornberg

Thank heaven
for BOOKS
and thank YOU
for READING!

Linda

Copyright © 2024 by Linda Hornberg

ISBN: 978-1-59849-360-3

Library of Congress Control Number: 2023919654

BISAC Codes:
GAR000000 GARDENING / General
GAR019050 GARDENING / Regional / Pacific Northwest (OR, WA)
JNF022000 JUVENILE NONFICTION / Gardening

Printed in China

www.pictureagarden.com
www.lindahornberg.com

Editor: Danielle Harvey
Proofreader: Ruthie Little
Layout: Soundview Design

All rights reserved. No part of this book may be transmitted
in any form or by any means, electronic or mechanical, including
photocopying, recording, or by any information storage or retrieval
system, in part, in any form, without the permission of the author.

Requests for such permissions should be addressed to:

Peanut Butter Publishing
Seattle, Washington 98102
206-860-4900
www.peanutbutterpublishing.com

This book is dedicated to Don Marshall,
Lake Washington's horticulture instructor extraordinaire,
family man, farmer, mentor, and mensch.
Kwanzan! Shirotae! Xylem! Phloem!

YOU HEARD IT HERE FIRST .

Foreword
by Lorene Edwards Forkner

Years ago, I was a young mother looking for a break from the daily toll of parenting, even if it meant standing at the end of a hose at the neighborhood nursery. I've been working in the gardening world ever since. I joke that my son drove me to a career in horticulture, but in fact the garden grew me into a better parent. Nurturing growth, watchful tending, and yes, even a bit of tedium, is how we raise our plants and our offspring.

By nature, kids are curious and eager to explore the world around them. Alongside daffodils, sunflowers, and pumpkins, a garden is fertile ground for cultivating wonder and responsibility. Among plants and pollinators, we find our place in a larger community, a web of life that may begin in the backyard but extends out into our neighborhoods and far beyond to all of Mother Earth.

Our world needs more gardeners. In some respects, growing the next generation of gardeners may be our most important harvest yet. *Picture A Garden* is a child's field guide to nature and an introduction to a world of amazement, where plants—and gardeners—play together. It's a story that's nearly as old as time yet remains as fresh as a sprouted seedling. Just as tending a garden is a continual learning process, *Picture A Garden* is a book that will grow along with kids and grownups of any age. Plus, everyone gets to play in the dirt.

Lorene Edwards Forkner writes the GROW column for *The Seattle Times*. She is the author of *Color In and Out of the Garden*, *Now is the Time For Trees*, and *The Beginner's Guide to Growing Great Vegetables*.

Acknowledgments

The author would like to thank Elliott Wolf of Peanut Butter Publishing for igniting the spark that set this passion project in motion. The manuscript was lovingly edited and proofread by Danielle Harvey and Ruthie Little. Amy Vaughn of Soundview Design worked her digital magic on my hand-inked typos and tipsy margins. The PBP team's feedback and moral support were greatly appreciated.

Love and gratitude are generously given to the formative influence of the families Hornberg-Rosenblatt, Watkins, Nagel, Balkin, Matz, Randall, Ellentuck, Haber, Sutton, Lempereur, and Liwerant. Additional families near and dear are Nickson, Kobe, Torres-Contreras, Barnett, Kamara, Avery, Gross, Lara-Jimenez, Paul, Bohacz, and Dowell. Too many art teachers to list, but Bob Sennhauser patiently taught me how to set hot type, and left a lasting impression—pun not entirely unintended. I have name-checked a few of you in the stories, but here's a shout out to the wonderful friends I made over my two decades at West Seattle Nursery. Waves and smiles to great neighbors who asked about progress and high-fived my chapter milestones as I passed by during daily dog walks. Thanks to my dogs for keeping the flab at bay while I spent entirely too many hours sitting down at the drawing board. Dr. Collins and crew at Burien Wellness unkinked my skeleton and massaged away the writer's cramp.

An affectionate nod goes to the New York boroughs of Manhattan and Brooklyn for brokering the marriages of Puerto Rico and the Ashkenaz, and seeding the fifty-two-years-long love story of Robert Avery Lara Hornberg and Florence Rosenblatt, my parents. ¡Wepa! and shalom to all.

Table of Contents

COME TO THE *OUTSIDE.*

WE HAVE SNACKS!

PICTURE A GARDEN

Who can garden? *you* can garden!

Plants and people make a delightful combination, and cultivating a fondness for nurturing green things can begin at any age. Gardening is a universally enjoyed activity, and while some aspects of raising plants can be physically challenging, it can also be quite fun. A garden is whatever you want it to be — whether you only have room for a few potted herbs or flowering marigolds on a windowsill, are only interested in growing food, or have the time and space to surround your home in a park-like forest. For most of us there are few ironclad rules dictating what you may plant, as long as you avoid introducing invasive weeds and keep branches and slippery fallen fruit off the sidewalks.

If you have never created a garden before, the best inspiration can often be found on a walk around your neighborhood. In the rare case that your new yard is mostly bare, you may feel overwhelmed by all of the empty space or lucky to have a blank canvas. Most gardeners begin with the laborious task of hacking down and winching out neglected old plants — too sorry to be saved — and countless, builder-installed boxwood hedges, half-dead junipers, prickly holly trees and "common-or-garden" (boring) foundation shrubs.

Your local garden center can be a good place to find supplies. A specialty nursery, small or large, will probably carry more unusual plants alongside the standard varieties, and is sure to have informative, green-thumbed plant people on staff to guide you. There is no such thing as a stupid plant question, and you will know more with every visit and every season in your garden. There is no such thing as a finished garden, either. You can always add (or remove) plants, as you discover new likes (and dislikes). Some plants will die. It's okay. There are so many things to learn and so many plants to love, and you can do that out in the fresh air and sunshine or from the comfort of your favorite chair. And you will make lots of new friends, as well — not just other gardeners, with whom you can exchange plants and ideas, but creatures with antennae, and wings, and furry tails, because they are all out there, waiting to welcome you into their world.

And that is where all good little cabbages come from.

Chapter One

How Did We Get Here?

The Origins of Species

Around the World in 80 Plants

As people migrated across the globe, so did plants. Some of those plants were carried along intentionally, valued as food or medicine. Others were nostalgic reminders of a distant homeland. 80 would be a very small fraction of the actual number of species introduced to new places. The word **exotic** means something novel, or previously unknown to a particular population. Every plant is well known somewhere.

Birds and other animals are active exporters of exotic plant species.

Sitka Spruce

There are vast timberlands up north, and the lumberyards are buzzing. Fir, Hemlock, Spruce and Pine are big in Canada.

They're not just for toast, and they weren't always available year-round!

Beyond the delicious Avocado, plants native to Central and South America include Cassava, Cashew and Carnauba. Eat the first two. Wax the car with the third one.

Farming is big, also in Canada, source of wheat, oats and barley crops.

True Native American plants:

"The Three Sisters"- corn, beans and squash

Florida oranges came from Asia

Maple sugar

Sisal for rope

Mexico: legendary source of all nightshades: potato, tomato & pepper! The Dutch took Mexican Cacao and turned it into the sweet chocolate we can't seem to get enough of.

Try some Maté, a South American tea alternative.

Plenty of potatoes here, too, in rainbow hues.

Hundreds of medicinal species come from South America's rainforests

Orchid heaven.

Small, tart crab apples are native to North America

Blueberry Cranberry Lingonberry - all thrive in New England's climate

over 800 varieties of mango grow in Puerto Rico

Love mango?

Hawaiian Pineapple began in Brazil, as did the Brazil Nut, rich in Strontium, for strong bones.

Ice plants are from Africa.

most of Iceland is too cold for crop cultivation, but hay grows well in the short summers. Hot-springs are used to heat greenhouses, and such imported species as grapes, tomatoes and even bananas can be grown there now.

Balsa! Rosewood! Mahogany! Life-saving quinine from Cinchona bark. Trees abound, and not only in the rainforests, which can claim 2,500 species.

Rubber was first used by natives in South America.

When you carry an ordinary, native plant from the environs of its origins and introduce it into foreign soil, it is considered exotic, no matter how plain its appearance may be to you. For thousands of years people moved plants and their seeds from place to place, not fully understanding the impact that non-natives can have on the local ecosystem. We are now much better informed about runaway invasives, and our governments regulate the commercial and civilian conveyance of plant matter, across borders and continents. This is why you are asked to declare the possession of plants in your luggage. No one wants to be the guy who holds up the line at the airport because of a forgotten banana in his carry-on. He's not in trouble because bananas are exotic — although they once were quite a new thing — but because agricultural products can harbor insect eggs, disease spores, or even live tarantulas under their skins. Better to be safe than sorry!

Plant introductions have improved soils and increased food security for many of the world's populations. We all appreciate some variety in our diet and the pleasure of discovering a new, amazingly flavorful fruit or herb. Collectors, or botanists who carried exotic samples back home as museum pieces or trophies, played a large role in putting ordinary plants from elsewhere "on the map".

Refrigeration and modern shipping modes guarantee that we can eat what were once "seasonal" crops nearly any time of the year.

"Have a nice cup of your "English" tea, and tip your hat to China, the home of the tea camellia."

"Scotch" Broom was first found in Normandy, France.

Birch, Beech, Oak and Aspen

Wild apples came from Europe and western Asia.

"Dutch" Tulips have their roots in Turkey.

Roots of the roots. Hardy beets, rutabagas, parsnips and turnips can withstand frigid northern winters, but grains grow well in summer.

A love of cabbage is cultivated way up here.

"Russian" Sage is from Afghanistan

Peony Land

There would be no English rose gardens, if not for ancient Persian and Chinese rose species.

Peanuts are not related to tree nuts, but they are legumes, like the pea.

So many of the plants we use and value came from Africa! Palm oil and Shea nut butter and, of course:

Ebony, mahogany and cork

Imagine life without wonderful spices!

More wonderful tea from India

The curry plant smells like curry, but is not the source of that delicious seasoning!

Most spice plants are not related to one another!

We prize exotic, ornamental plants, but humans have always been excited to try food crops from faraway. Early voyages of discovery were largely driven by the quest for foods and spices.

Dates and olives and papyrus reed

Thank Africa for Coffee beans

Coffee, tea and sugar can take the subtropical heat, but it is too much for most food crops.

The Hevea tree, source of latex for making rubber, grows throughout the Tropics, but demand for latex production fell heavily on African laborers, once automobiles created a need for rubber tires.

Rice is the world's most widely eaten grain crop. So much of the planet's food is exported, and there never seems to be enough to meet the needs of the most densely populated regions.

Silk is made by larvae that feed on the Mulberry tree.

Leptospermum, or "Tea Tree," is only one of many Aussie natives we adore.

Beans Talk

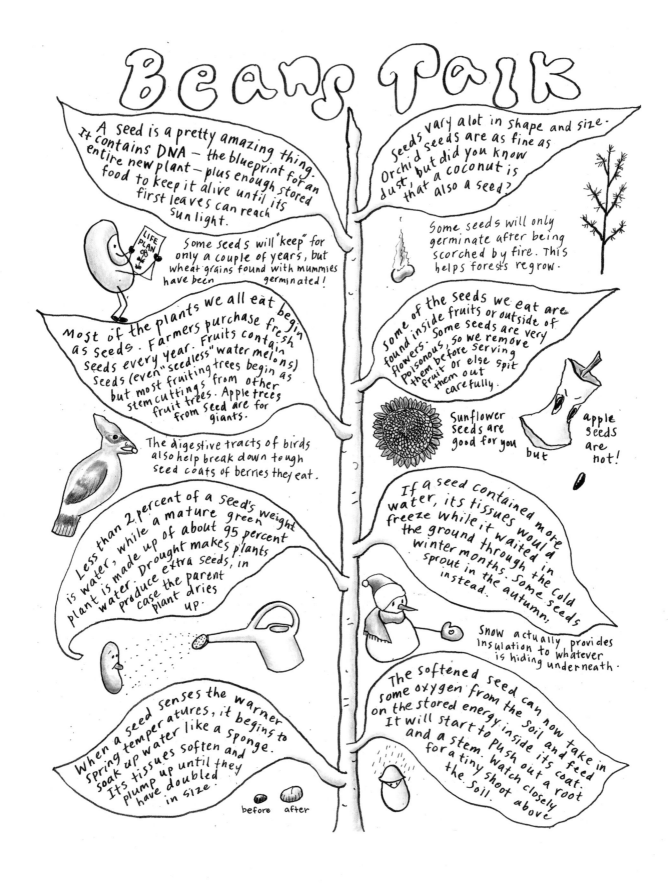

A seed is a pretty amazing thing. It contains DNA – the blueprint for an entire new plant – plus enough stored food to keep it alive until its first leaves can reach sunlight.

LIFE PLAN

Some seeds will "keep" for only a couple of years, but wheat grains found with mummies have been germinated!

Seeds vary a lot in shape and size. Orchid seeds are as fine as dust, but did you know that a coconut is also a seed?

Some seeds will only germinate after being scorched by fire. This helps forests regrow.

Most of the plants we all eat begin as seeds. Farmers purchase fresh seeds every year. Fruits contain seeds (even "seedless" water melons) but most fruiting trees begin as stem cuttings from other fruit trees. Apple trees from seed are for giants.

Some of the seeds we eat are found inside fruits or outside of flowers. Some seeds are very poisonous, so we remove them before serving fruit or else spit them out carefully.

The digestive tracts of birds also help break down tough seed coats of berries they eat.

Sunflower seeds are good for you

but

apple seeds are not!

Less than 2 percent of a seed's weight is water, while a mature green plant is made up of about 95 percent water. Drought makes plants produce extra seeds, in case the parent plant dries up.

If a seed contained more water, its tissues would freeze while it waited in the ground through the cold winter months. Some seeds sprout in the autumn, instead.

Snow actually provides insulation to whatever is hiding underneath.

When a seed senses the warmer spring temperatures, it begins to soak up water like a sponge. Its tissues soften and plump up until they have doubled in size.

before   after

The softened seed can now take in some oxygen from the soil and feed on the stored energy inside its coat. It will start to push out a root and a stem. Watch closely for a tiny shoot above the soil.

and sow it begins...

the map of life inside a seed.

Snoozing away the winter.

Is that a chickadee? My singing alarm clock!

Sun and rain are equally appreciated.

Tough seed coat

Tender seed leaf

A cotyledon is the embryonic leaf of a plant, chiefly made of starch and oil.

Dicots have two **seed leaves**, and regardless of the type of plant, whether it will turn out to be a petunia or a hazelnut tree, cotyledons look remarkably alike. The second set of leaves to sprout will be the **true leaves**, and those are the ones we can use to help identify what is growing.

A single seed leaf will emerge from a monocot seed. A blade of grass is a good example.

DICOT

Most of our **broad**-leaved plants are dicots, from peas and beans to rosebushes and apple trees.

MONOCOT

Corn, grasses, lilies, irises and tulips are monocots.

Most **conifers** — trees with cones — put out multiple seed leaves. They are called **polycotyledons**.

Beet seeds are packaged stuck together, which gives them an unusual shape.

Some plants have very distinctive seeds, but its wise to hold onto your packets until you are ready to plant.

You can plant nuts in the shell, or not bother, because the squirrels will kindly do it for you!

Your dog will happily bring home seeds with prickly burrs.

A **coconut** is probably the largest seed you will ever see, and though it is heavy, it can float into the water and float to shore before sprouting into a new palm tree. Plenty of bigger trees come from smaller seeds.

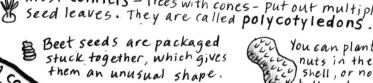

Winged seeds, like maple samaras travel just fine on the breeze.

Some seed pods go pop when they are ripe, and can send their seeds quite a distance.

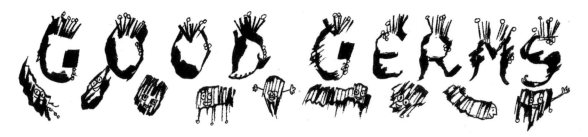

GOOD GERMS

Micro organisms are the tiny critters we can only see through the magnification of a microscope. They are responsible for infecting us with contagious diseases, but also for helping us digest what we ingest. When we are enjoying a spoonful of yogurt with active cultures, we are introducing beneficial bacteria into our gut flora ~ the tiny, busy zoo inside our bellies. Plants thrive when the right microbes are present in the soil, and soil devoid of beneficial fungi produces stunted plant growth.

Colonies of mycorrhizal fungi attach themselves to plant roots and **fix**, or pre-digest nitrogen.

Soil microbes are not the type of active cultures you want to eat, so always wash your hands well before eating.

yumbo WHEAT GERM

Approved.

Who put the germ in **germination?** When a dormant seed springs to life, we say it has germinated. Sometimes ideas are referred to as germs, as though a project or invention grew out of a tiny seed in somebody's brain. Have you ever eaten wheat germ? It doesn't sound particularly appetizing, but it is actually one of the most nutritious parts of a wheat seed, or berry. **Whole** wheat bread leaves the bran intact, so your slice of unbleached, nutty bread delivers you more value per bite. Try some different kinds of bread. There are delicious varieties baked from mixed, whole grain flours (wheat, plus oat and rye). Some have whole seeds baked inside or decorating the crust: poppy, sesame, caraway, sunflower. If your body doesn't tolerate **gluten**, there are breads made from millet, amaranth, rice and nut flours. Sprouted bread is made using grains that have already germinated. You can't see little green sprouts in your toast, but if that is disappointing, try growing some beansprouts in a jar.

What about those plants that don't reproduce by seed? Ferns and mosses start from tiny **spores**. Many beautiful flowers grow from **bulbs**, **tubers**, **corms** and **rhizomes**, which are larger than flower seeds.

Eureka!

I just figured out what I wanna grow up to be!

Some of their flowers also produce seeds, but flowerbulbs are famous for **multiplying** by **division**. That's not a tricky math problem. They produce **offsets**, which can be separated from mom. Divide and conquer

The Adventures of an Adventitious Root

Roots are the generally unseen, unglamorous and often unconsidered parts of a plant. They tend to spend their time underground, only drawing our attention when they interfere with our ability to dig, push up a slab of the sidewalk, or — worst of all — break into a sewer pipe. Without roots, however, no plant would be able to pull water up from the soil, plants would blow away and trees would topple. For certain species, the root is the plant part we value almost exclusively, and root crops like carrots, turnips, parsnips and rutabagas have fed populations for millennia.

When we buy those adorable little tumbled baby carrots, they've been shorn of their green, leafy locks (Grandma used them as soup greens!) and wispy root hairs.

Potato tubers are plump, starchy roots with eyes in the back of their heads (and fronts, too) out of which plants sprout.

root hairs

Vascular bundles
Cross-section shows how a root transports water upward and food downward.

These roots are all out-of-sight, under the soil, but there is something **astonishing** that plants can do, which would be kind of like you having the ability to grow an extra **ear** on your **elbow**. Plants can grow roots **adventitiously**, which means from locations where roots would not normally need to grow. This gives them another way to reproduce, by effectively **cloning** themselves from a branch or leaf.

Go on, Mrs. Blabinsky— I'm listening!

If you make a small cut in an African Violet leaf and pin it to moist soil with a piece of wire, roots will sprout from the cut.

root buds

It's easy to spot **aerial** root starts on some plants, but even where they are absent, roots can be encouraged to grow at any leaf **node** with the help of a bit of rooting **hormone** powder.

Cutting remarks: most **woody** nursery stock is produced through the use of cloned stem cuttings. Starting plants from cuttings has a long history, and many a favorite tree or shrub has been brought along to a new home as a **slip**, or small piece of a branch. Keep your cutting in water or with the cut end wrapped in a damp paper towel until you can get it into a pot of soil to grow roots.

SEDUM·no·SEED·UM

or, THERE ARE MORE WAYS THAN ONE TO HATCH AN EGGPLANT.

Propagation is a big word that means making more of any living thing. Plants make more plants each year on their own, without our help, but we tend to like some plants better than others, so we encourage them to propagate. Opening up a brightly colored seed packet, or shaking the dried seed head of a spent poppy or columbine is an easy way to make more of our flowering favorites. Seeds develop after flowers have been pollinated by wind or insects, and most are ripe by the end of the summer. Nearly all plants produce some kind of flower — not necessarily showy — but not all flowers produce **viable** seeds, or seeds that can produce more flowering plants. Seeds that you eat will not grow plants inside your tummy. Seeds eaten by birds will grow new plants, but not inside the bird's tummy. Birds will pass them, in flight, along with nutrient-rich droppings for your soil. The new plants they have gifted to you will not always be your flowering favorites, strategically or aesthetically placed. When you say, "Hmm. I don't remember planting Mountain Ash there," suspect a friendly bird. Then pluck out the Mountain Ash. It won't have room.'

Poppies, columbines and Nigella have balloon-like seed pods you can shake once dried

crimson stem

COLUMBINE.

Cloning is the process of reproducing plants by **vegetative** means. Cloning methods bypass pollen exchange and seed production. A rooted **cutting** taken from a hybridized designer **cultivar** will grow a new plant with identical characteristics. A **cultivar** can be recognized by a capitalized name in single quotes on the plant label. The plant has been enhanced to feature more impressive blooms, improved fruit size and flavor or disease resistance. Seed from a cultivar will either be **sterile** — not capable of germination — or it will sprout a plant which won't resemble the cultivar. New cultivars create a sensation in the gardening world. They also tend to be expensive, because the new plant and its cultivar **name** are patented, trade marked creations. Sometimes it is worthwhile to wait a couple of years before investing in the latest sensation. Some cultivars turn out to be genetically unstable, and the two-headed, repeat-blooming, variegated plaid super plant you paid so much to acquire **reverts** to the common wildflower of its humble origin. You can take a small stem cutting from Mom's 'Peace' rose, root it and plant it. Don't set up shop and plan to sell your cuttings — that would be illegal. Also, Mom's 'Peace' was grafted onto a root stock, so your clone may perform somewhat differently. Do it for fun. (And cloning **IS** fun!)

you will not get this → from seed.

Rosa 'Peace' is one of the world's most popular Hybrid Tea Roses. A 'Peace' rose will always have soft, pink-blushed, yellow petals.

Sedums work well in living walls – vertical gardens. You can also tuck them into wreaths made with sphagnum moss.

NEED MORE SEDUM? PULL SOME FROM MUM!

We're all CLONES of happy SEDUM Mom had SEEDS, but We don't NEED 'um!

The Jade plant is a tropical relative of Sedum. Both come from the Crassulaceae family. Jades are drought-tolerant houseplants with thick, fleshy leaves. You can also clone a Jade from a leaf.

← HEN
← CHICK

Sempervivum, or Hens and chicks are another succulent you can clone.

Cropping Stonecrops

Cropping Stonecrops is one of the easiest ways to make more plants. The common name for Sedum is stonecrop. Many species of Sedum have leaves that resemble pebbles, but their low watering requirements also make them like living stones. Each green pebble is a leaf, which can root if it lands on soil and start a whole new plant. The leaves are **succulent**, or juicy — they carry a water supply like a cactus does. This gives a leaf the ability to stay alive for weeks between rains, or in your pocket (check before you do laundry). There are so many colorful varieties of stonecrops, and they propagate so easily that you can collect them all and trade them with your friends. If you are not the best at remembering to water, these are the perfect plants for you. Did I mention that they flower? They do, and in some amazing, neon colors!

Sedum 'Angelina' is a prolific, needle-leaved spreader, in bright, yellow-green.

S. pachyphyllum is also called the jelly-bean plant. Its green leaves have a touch of pink.

S. acre has extra texture. Its ambitious nature is in its name — it spreads vigorously.

S. spathufolium is so-named because of its spoony, curved leaves. This species has many popular varieties. My favorite is S. spathufolium 'Cape Bianco' whose leaves form small chalky blue-green rosettes.

'Dragon's Blood' is a tall spoon-leaved Sedum. It has leaves of deep, shiny green, reddish stems and hot pink flowerheads.

S. album has dainty white blooms held on wispy stalks above small pebbles.

S. 'Button' has the tiniest leaves. ○ It ○ is ○ too ○ cute ○ for ○ words ○ ACTUAL SIZE! So ○ I ○ will ○ say ○ no ○ more ○ about ○ Sedum ○

Solanum lycopersicum

"The Love Apple"

or, what's in a name?

Alas,
young 'Romeo' is a
Plum tomato.
Fair 'Juliet' is a
Grape tomato.

'Though both are the same, botanically,
their feuding clans will never agree.

"Toe-may-toe — Toe-mah-toe —
what's the difference?" you scoff.
Before things get messy,
Let us call the whole thing off.

Chapter Two

What's in a Name?
The Language of Plants

HELLO

MY NAME IS ...

DAISY, DAISY, give me your answer, do! I'm half crazy, trying to remember you! And, it's no small feat to attempt a census count of the world's daisy population. The Daisy Family, known scientifically as **COMPOSITAE***, is the largest family of annual, biennial and perennial plants. It is divided botanically into more than a dozen **tribes**, for ease of identification. All daisies are formed of a disk (or disc) center, where seed will form, and a secondary arrangement of showy rays, the petals traditionally plucked while one ponders dear Daisy's fickle affections. **Single** daisies sport a simple row of rays. **Double** daisies can have so many rays that the central disk is concealed under a pom-pom. (There are no **Married** daisies. Perhaps there would simply be too many relatives to invite to the wedding.) Many families hold an **Annual** reunion each year. **Annual** plants do not make it through to the following summer, so the **Marigold** which has popped up in your lettuce bed this year is an offspring from seed dropped by last year's marigold. It has no memory of last year's marigold's potato salad or high-pitched laugh, but it may look remarkably similar, and will respond to the same name. In place of the family barbecue, then, let's send our flowery composite clan to the **Annual Daisy Convention**, where they will meet all of their cousins, for the first time (just like last year, and two years ago, and ten years ago).

↑ this ray petal is actually a flower

A **composite** head. whether she loves you or loves you not, every daisy has a central **disk** surrounded by a ring of colorful, nectar-less **rays**, two distinct flower types.

GRAND BALLROOM

ASTER TRIBE : Register at this booth if you are a **Lazy** Daisy, **Tahoka** Daisy, **Swan River** Daisy, **English** Daisy, **Kingfisher** Daisy. **China** Asters also invited!

ANTHEMIS TRIBE : This is the spot if you are a **Marguerite**, a **Palm Springs**, a **Cobbity** Daisy. Welcoming all of our annual **Mum** and **Feverfew** cousins.

I'm Brachy come, a Swan River!

Kingfisher, here. Call me Felicia!

I'm Matricaria, a Feverfew. You must be Marguerite— you look just like my cousin Argyranthemum!

Close -- I'm Cobbity, an Argeranthemum. There's some argy-bargy about the spelling.

Note the ASTERISK! ⟶ * ALSO KNOWN AS **ASTERACEAE**, SINCE THE TREND OF RE-NAMING ALL FAMILIES FOR ONE GENUS. ALL ASTERS ARE COMPOSITES, BUT NOT ALL COMPOSITES ARE ASTERS — OR ARE THEY ???

SAHARA ROOM

SAFARI ROOM

HELIANTHUS TRIBE: The place for Gloriosa Daisy, Tickseed, Zinnia, Cosmos, Dahlia, and our famous kin, the Sunflower.

ARCTOTIS TRIBE: Come on in, if you are an African Daisy, Namaqualand Daisy, or Treasure Flower. Strawflowers, too!

I'm Rudbeckia, a Gloriosa, but you can call me Becky!

May I ask for an autograph?

My pleasure, Becky! Helianthus, at your beck and call!

Osteo-spermum, that's me! I'm an African.

Call me, Gazania.

I'm a Treasure, to some!

Mid-day Mixer out on

Feelin' HOT · HOT · HOT!

Annual! Perennial! It's a party!
THE SUN DECK

Hot, Sun & Cool drinks

Artichoke dip and Endive will not be on the menu!

CARDUUS TRIBE
Thistle be our best year, ever!

I'm Echinops, or Globe Thistle

Centaurea, an annual, perennial Bachelor, it seems!

HELENIUM TRIBE
Blanket Flower, Sneezeweed

Helenium, here. I'm not contagious, I promise!

EUPATORIUM TRIBE
Boneset, Agrimony, Floss Flower, Blazing Star

Ageratum, the Floss Flower.

I'm a Boneset, or Eupatorium.

Call me Joe Pye!

CALENDULA TRIBE
Cape Marigold, Pot Marigold

No one would guess we Calendula were Annuals!

VERNONIA TRIBE
Goldenrod, Yarrow

CICHORIUM TRIBE
Cupid's Dart, Chicory, Hawkweed

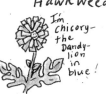

I'm Chicory— the Dandy-lion in blue!

Catananche

INULA TRIBE
Strawflower, Pearly Everlasting, Immortelle

Heli-chrysum, Straw flower!

Our lives are brief, but we keep for ages!

Rhodanthe, Everlasting!

Shhh— I'm Achillea, the Yarrow. I'm really from the Anthemis tribe, but I look more Vernonian!

well, it is kind of lonely being a goldenrod. Name's Solidago!

SENECIO TRIBE
Leopard's Bane, Dusty Miller, Arnica Ligularia, Tassel Flower

(Emilia, the Tassel and Cineraria, the Dusty, have gone off to powder their noses.)

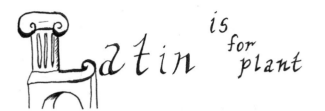 

Latin is for plant Lovers.

Rosa is Latin for **red**, or, considering the fact that Latin is older than English, we could say that **red** is English for **rosa**. New words are added to the English vocabulary all the time, some of them newly "coined", to name new concepts or inventions. Others are borrowed or adopted from other languages. About half of the words we consider to be English ones derive directly from classical Latin (alumni, bacteria, podium) or indirectly, from Old French, one of several **Romance** languages, which share Latin roots. The linguistic similarity can be seen in the words flor, fleur, fiore and flower, from **flos**. Latin itself doesn't sound nearly as **romantic** as Spanish, French or Italian. What it does sound like, however, is science, and that is because so many of our scientific terms are Latin. The Romans, whose mighty empire gave us the Alphabet as we recognize it today — adapted from the letter forms of the Greeks, who adapted it from the Phoenecians, who adapted it from the Semites, who adapted it from the Egyptians — simply had more power and influence.

Carolus Linnaeus is the Latin name of the Swedish botanist, Karl von Linné. He became a naturalist and a professor, but is most well-known for giving us a uniform and universal system for naming and classifying plants and animals. He chose Latin, and set out to organise every known organism with a **genus**, for the group to which it belonged, followed by a **species** name, for a unique — or **specific** — member of that group.

Did Karl—or Carolus—stop to smell the roses? We can make a guess, based on some of the names shared with other fragrant flowers, such as Rosa dianthiflora, which looks like a Dianthus (carnation). Of course, he probably named that, also.

Species names — if not made to honor the plant's namer, their best friend or their long lost love — are largely of a descriptive nature. They reflect the color, texture or shape of some part of the plant, often its leaf type.

LINEAR — SHAPED LIKE A LINE.

A LANCEOLATE LEAF, SHAPED LIKE A LANCE, OR SWORD.

A PALMATE LEAF, SHAPED LIKE A PALM, OR HAND.

AN OVATE LEAF, SHAPED LIKE AN OVAL, OR EGG.

OBLONGATE— SHAPED LIKE AN OBLONG.

Latin plant names can be memorized. You dont have to study Latin itself. It is helpful to learn the universally recognized names for the plants you love, because common names can be regional, and are sometimes applied to more than one plant. Pronunciation? Now that's a separate adventure in communication! (The correct pronunciation for my favorite flowering vine may be **clem-uh-tiss**, but I cant help being stuck on clem-**aah**-tiss.)

D'yall have any MAYPOPS?

IT TOOK A FEW MINUTES AND A THOROUGH DESCRIPTION UNTIL I UNDERSTOOD THAT THIS TEXAN WAS LOOKING FOR A PASSIONFLOWER, OR **Passiflora**.

Flora & Fauna

The Dingaling Bros. Circus has just come to town. Every animal in its performing menagerie has a name that can be found in the plant world. In this case, the names we are looking for are not scientific ones, but common or folk names. You probably know some of the plants. Find their names and look for the namesake animals showing off their talents. Admission is free!

POPCORN · TAFFY APPLES · FROZEN CUSTARD
RED HOTS · COTTON CANDY · PRETZELS · SODA
PLEASE DON'T TOSS PE___S _ TO THE ANI

Chelone- TURTLE HEAD

Fragaria 'PINK PANDA'
Leonotis- LION'S EAR
Campanula- HAREBELL
Geranium- CRANE'S BILL

Faucaria- TIGER'S JAWS

Erigeron- FLEA BANE

Doronicum- LEOPARD'S BANE
Araucaria- MONKEY PUZZLE TREE

Lysimachia- GOOSENECK LOOSESTRIFE
Erythronium- DOG'S TOOTH VIOLET
Polygonatum- SOLOMON'S SEAL
Rubus- SALMON BERRY
Tacca- CAT'S WHISKERS
Bergenia- ELEPHANT'S EARS
Armoracia- HORSERADISH
Hibbertia- SNAKE VINE
Lysichiton- SKUNK CABBAGE

Acanthus- BEAR'S BREECHES
Antirrhinum- SNAPDRAGON

You know, I was the original Bearded Lady!

Aruncus- GOAT'S BEARD

17

BACK TO SCHOOL

BOTANY

An apple for the teacher

A is for apple. That is the first fact we learn when we are introduced to the alphabet. A crisp, shiny apple makes a nice gift for your teacher, who is probably glad it's not another mug (with a picture of an apple on it — teachers have a cupboard filled with those). The plump, sweet apples we can buy today came along to our shores from far away, but they also came a long way, through hybridization, from the small, sour fruits of **Malus sylvestris**. That's the botanical name for apple.

> I think that I shall never see
> A poem as lovely as an apple tree

Fruit seeds travel by various means to reach their new homes.

The Latin for fruit is **carp**. One of my snack favorites... carp, that is — not fruit.

Apples fall into the group known as **pome** fruits, but a pomegranate is not a pome.

Carpels are juicy segments separated by **carpel walls**, which make me think of wall-to-wall carpets...

The upright apple blossom flops over after it's been pollinated, so the developing apple hangs upside-down! Bees must transfer pollen between two different hybrids.

No bloom? No bees? No sweet, juicy apple!

← flower remnant

You can eat the skin, even if it's been waxed.

↳ endocarp
↳ mesocarp
↳ exocarp

Backyard apples have a bad reputation for harboring "worms". Cut into your homegrown fruit. If you see this   or   this

codling moth larva

Apple maggot-fly larva

you should visit your local plant nursery for pest management advice and non-toxic remedies.

The three barely perceptible layers of the **pericarp** — the edible part of the apple. Don't eat the core, no matter how yummy it is, unless you spit out all the seeds.

The BERRY is the most varied — and surprising — fruit group. Surely a berry must be smaller than a POME, such as an apple, pear or quince! Guess what: a melon — even a watermelon bigger than a breadbox — is a type of berry called a PEPO. It has to do with the type of seeds and their arrangement. A pepo's seeds are flat, oval in shape and slippery. They are randomly arranged inside the pericarp. In muskmelons — like cantaloupe and crenshaw — they are easily scooped out of the center, after you cut the fruit in half. This will not work with a watermelon, whose seeds are less centralized. Seedless watermelons have unripe seeds, which takes the fun out of seed-spitting contests. If your vision of eating berries involves having a bowl full of them, try growing some cucamelons. They are also known as Mexican Sour gherkins, although they are not that sour. They are the size of a grape.

A traditional watermelon

Personal size

A traditional watermelon seed.

← actual size!

Cantaloupe, a **pepo** berry, with its centrally-located, asymmetrical seed cluster. My child requested this "regular melon", after I brought home a weird, green-fleshed honeydew.

Have a yummy bowl of cucamelons (a.k.a. mouse melons), but hold the whipped cream.

Vitamin C!

Any citrus fruit is a **hesperidium**, a juice-filled, pulpy berry whose interior is divided into segments. The skin, or rind contains a fragrant oil which will mist and clean stale air when you peel it off. The peel is edible but bitter.

A thin slice of citrus looks like a stained glass window.

An **aggregate** berry is made up of a cluster of tiny **drupes**, each containing a seed.

you can cook and eat young grape leaves

this one will be extremely sour.

Raspberry, marionberry, blackberry, boysenberry — they are all soft fruits. They are delicate to ship, easily bruised and tricky to store, but even when overripe, they all make excellent jams and pies.

Grapes are simple berries which tend to be high in sugar content. For some reason, it became customary to bring grapes when visiting someone in the hospital.

a grape has pear-shaped seeds, unless it happens to be a seedless grape. It is much easier to eat if it is seedless. Too many will give you a bellyache.

You can add a ton of sugar to lemon juice and make lemonade, or to orange peel to make marmalade. Or, you can just eat an orange! Satsumas are sweet little easy to peel, great-smelling tangerines. No biting into a bitter rind to get them started.

Stone fruits, such as plums, cherries, nectarines, apricots, and peaches, are properly known as **drupes**. At their core is a hard shell, containing a single, toxic seed. Don't eat the seeds — they are The Pits.

A coffee "bean" is the seed found inside a berry of the Coffea plant. The pulp of the berry has no value, but millions worship the bean on a daily basis.

That's right, a banana is also a berry.

It's not at all juicy, and comes wrapped in a weird, rubbery peel. A popular snack for all ages.

FOCUS ON the FAMILY

Scientific classification groups organisms together based on their physical similarities and reproductive compatibility. The names given to individuals within a particular group can sound vastly different, yet those creatures, plants or rocks are closely related to the others in their group. In an animal family, biologists refer to those whose dietary habits, overall appearance, and perhaps sleep preferences are shared. Plant family members also share outer characteristics, but often the resemblance can only be observed up close, in a tiny part of the plant, such as the arrangement of petals.

This can be your ancestry — your parents, their parents, going back for endless generations in time,

the Family Tree

or, it could be a favorite tree, planted by a grandparent and still there at the old family homestead.

the Tree Family

This one would have to be a colony of related trees growing together, perhaps as seedlings of the same parent tree. Scientifically, there is no such tree **family**!

It would seem to make much simpler sense if all trees were in the same family — after all, they are tall, have trunks, bark, branches and leaves — and also if all flowers made up a flower family, vines a vine family and fruits a fruit family. That is not, however, how classification works. Trees fall into many families, and most of those families also include a wide range of other, smaller plants. It makes sense — mostly — if you take a close look at their leaves and flowers. Let's try:

Leguminosae, or **Fabaceae** (the names occasionally change, just to keep things interesting...)

the Pea Family

This amazing clan includes all of your beans, lentils and peas, and also Wisteria vines. Trees related to peas include such beauties as Redbud (Cercis), Mimosa (Albizzia) and Golden Chain (Laburnum). Black Locust (Robinia) and Honey Locust (Gleditsia), Scotch Broom (Cytisus) and Clover (Trifolium) all have the same flower shape, though they vary considerably in size. The trees and vines make pods with beans inside, but never eat them because they are poisonous. Stick to your delicious cowpeas!

Rosaceae
Roses get top billing, but any person from Japan can tell you the importance of cherry blossom viewing, when the world snows in pink!

the Rose Family

Even if you never plant a rosebush, it is next to impossible to find a garden that excludes the rose family. So many edible fruits ~ Apple (Malus), Pear (Pyrus), Peach (Persica), Quince (Cydonia), Plum (Prunus) and cherries (also Prunus) ~ are rose cousins. Native roses fruit, too, and these hips are high in vitamin C. There are too many ornamentals in this family to list here, but they are everywhere. Just step outside!

Kingdom: *Animalia* = animal, not vegetable or mineral.

C Phyllum: *Chordata* = possessing a central spinal cord.

L Subphyllum: *Vertebrata* = supported by a flexible, bony spine.

A Class: *Mammalia* = gives birth to live young, fed on its own milk.

S Order: *Carnivora* = primary food requirement is meat.

S Family: *Felidae* = includes every type of **feline**, or cat.

Genus: *Felis* = small cats least likely to devour Homo sapiens.

Species: ***domesticus*** = house-trainable companion or pet.

(the Cat Family)

I FICATON. A cat is a class act, who likes to believe she is head of the class. Cats spend most of their time feeling important — or at least, dreaming about their position in the pecking order. All cats are related to one another, at least distantly, whether or not they decide to acknowledge any other feline, or any living thing in the room, which they are certain to do to maintain their pride.

Many of us enjoy living domestically with *Felis domesticus*, the **Family Cat**. We also like to observe their larger, undomesticated relatives, but from a safe distance, and on the other side of a sturdy fence, pane of glass, or other reliable physical barricade.

Let's take a peek at ⧙ *Felidae* ⧙ and some Big Cats.

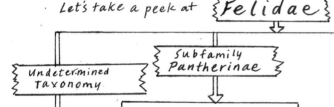

Undetermined Taxonomy

Subfamily Pantherinae

subfamily Felinae

Cheetahs

Long, lean running machine, achieving speeds of up to 56 miles per hour. It can chase prey or run faster than any predator.

Panthera Group
Includes, of course, the Panther, but shares close DNA patterns with these:
Lion · Tiger · Leopard · Snow Leopard · Jaguar · Lynx · Caracal · Ocelot · Bobcat · Serval · Bay Cat · Jaguarundi · Clouded Leopard · Puma · Ounce · Irimote cat · Fishing Cat · Flat-headed Cat · Rusty Spotted Cat · Marbled Cat · Asian Golden Cat.

Ocelots
Rarely seen (but always spotted). They are shy and avoid populated areas. The Ocelot group includes, besides its namesake, the Pampas Cat · Kod Kod · Geoffroy's cat. Andean Mountain cat · Margay · Oncilla. Should you chance to encounter **any** Big Cat, decline lunch invitations and resist the selfie.

Wild Cats
The largest of the Wild Cat Group is the Jungle Cat, up to 35 pounds. Our domestic cats most likely descend from the African Wild Cat. Others are Pallas's Cat · Black-footed Cat · Chinese Desert Cat · Jungle Cat.

Seven... six... five...

Silvi enjoys **being a pet**, the many benefits of which include regular meals, shelter from the elements, the attention an alpha demands and her choice of many warm and cushioned nap spots. She occasionally enjoys **being petted**, but if you keep it up for too long, she will bite the hand that feeds her. She cannot enjoy **being pet**. That is bad grammar.

Found as a young, pregnant stray, Silvi gave birth to an astonishing litter of **ten** kittens. Following that event, I took her into the vet to be **spayed**, so that would not happen ever again. She was not **spade** or **spaded**. Garden beds, and not **pets** are **spaded**, with a **spade**.

The Better to Smell You With, My Dear.

The enormous volcanic stone statues on Easter Island — or **Rapa Nui**, as it is known by the people of the same name, represent their ancestors, who arrived at least five hundred, but possibly over one thousand years earlier. The native name for the figures is **Moai**, and although some of them were toppled, for reasons unknown — and through a Herculean effort — dozens of others continue to stand silent watch over the island. According to the spoken lore of their descendants, the founding immigrants, led by their chief, **Hotu Matúa**, sailed from another Pacific island, Hiva, in canoes filled with livestock, food and water supplies, and cuttings of familiar plants. After a two-month long, one-way voyage, they established a home on Rapa Nui. Anthropologists are still trying to determine why their civilization appears to have collapsed and their attempts at sustaining agricultural food supplies failed, but the small remnant of this adventuring population point to the combined factors of sub-tropical climate, warfare with competing inhabitants, and the arrival of later explorers, who couldn't make sense of their culture.

THE NOSE KNOWS. The Rapa Nui used a form of pictographic writing called **petroglyphs**, or symbols carved into rock. The earliest known forms of written language were recorded in this way — "written in stone", or impressed into clay — until paper was invented. Paper takes its name from **Papyrus**, a marsh reed plant whose stems were soaked and flattened by the ancient Egyptians, laid side by side to dry and beaten into sheets. Documents written on paper scrolls are easier to transport than stone and clay tablets, and the portability of paper advanced civilization, promoting the exchange of information and ideas. The **oral tradition** — the memorization of stories and ritual details — is still an essential part of countless cultures. Another important piece of cultural memory is **fragrance**, and the cultivation of plants that were not grown as food indicates the importance people placed on **smell**.

A Nose by any other Name still smells the same.

Nose, nariz, nez, schnozz... all smell, equally well. Noses bring in the aromas which help us to taste our food. They say taste is personal — well, so is smell! Smells can be cultural, and coming across a familiar or forgotten scent from long ago can send you instantly back to childhood or transport you to a faraway land. A perfume that draws one person in for a deeper whiff can make the next person swoon and run for fresh air. There are colognes that remind you of your third grade teacher, and cleaning products that evoke a long-gone building. It's kind of like having time in a bottle.

Does it remind you a little bit of a grenade? If you are allergic or simply averse to perfumes concocted in cosmetics labs, then this puffer bottle is a literal stink bomb.

Eau de Luxe

Flowers have scent to help attract bees and other pollinators.

Dracunculus, the Dragon Lily smells like rotten meat.

Some of the most cloying (choke-y) and foul-smelling flowers are pollinated by flies rather than bees. There is no accounting for taste.

Humans have long taken advantage of plant-derived fragrances to disguise unpleasant odors on the body and in the home. Before the advent of indoor plumbing — and water heaters — baths were very infrequent. Flooring was old, musty boards, if you were lucky, or swept, compacted earth. People would **strew**, or sprinkle herbs on the floor and in bedding, not only to relieve the nostrils, but also to kill lice and other crawly houseguests. The common names of many plants we still value today contain hints to their one-time value as strewing herbs, soap-making ingredients, or as other vital household helpers.

Lavandula, commonly known as Lavender, whose Latin name derived from **lavo** – to wash

Now with volcanic pumice!

Artemisia, or wormwood, named for the Greek goddess of the hunt. A potent vermifuge, or dewormer.

Aromatherapy and Homeopathy also go way back. Early medicine relied on using plant essences, tinctures, oils and compresses, which aided in stimulating various organ functions, relaxing muscles, healing wounds and relieving pain. Ailing English village folk sought herbal remedies formulated in the monasteries. Perhaps if King Henry VIII had been less hasty about booting out the monks, they might have treated the painful leg ulcers from which he suffered at the end of his reign.

YOUR  ANNUAL REVIEW

Thanks for coming, everyone.

It's time to take stock of our futures.

Pansy's the big thinker. I prefer to live in the moment!

Does this guy not know we'll be going to seed in a few months? Should I stay mum?

That's fine for you, Sweet William. You young biennials can wait 'til next year to get serious.

Things smell pretty sweet to me, even if they don't look rosy...

I'm Impatiens. I can't wait for next year.

ANNUALS are planted **ANNUALLY**. An annual starts from seed, germinates in about a week, blooms its heart out for months, until it is bloomed out. Once it is tired of all that, an annual plans for the end of its brightly colored life by setting seed for next year's generation. In seed form, it has no winter cares. They are worth the repeat investment.

BIENNIALS live for two years, but typically save their flower performance for year two. Leave those roots in the ground for winter. — the top will return!

PERENNIALS live for multiple years, and some will become woody, while others have green stems which die back over winter. Their bloom time tends to be briefer than an annual or a biennial's show, but there is less re-planting.

Name That Petunia!

Violet, Rose, Daisy, Lily, Magnolia, Hortense, Petunia, Iris, Marigold, Poppy, Dahlia, Hyacinth. They sound old-fashioned, but they'll probably come back, as young parents look for something new and different to name their babies. Before these became popular names for little girls — and they were once quite common — they were names for flowers. Flowers, of course, were named by people, and some flowers were named for people. Is there some one you can think of whose name comes from a flower? Veronica, maybe, or Erica or Daphne? Boys also got some plant names, but they tended to be less perfumed. Let's visit the **Nursery** for newborns, and see how many plants we find!

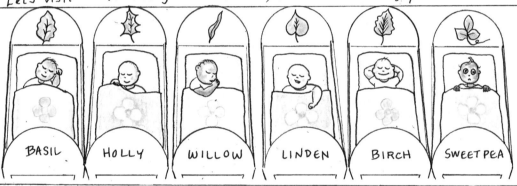

BASIL　　HOLLY　　WILLOW　　LINDEN　　BIRCH　　SWEET PEA

. Look at the little darlings, all sleeping so peacefully. Oh — except for Sweet Pea, who may be thinking, "They're not *seriously* going to call me *that*, are they?" Relax, baby Sweet Pea. Perhaps they will give you the scientific equivalent, **Lathyrus**, instead, and include your middle name, **Odoratus** at diaper changes, or whenever you behave like a little stinker! Actually, the species name, odoratus is meant as praise for the much-loved fragrance of the sweet pea blossom. I personally prefer the herbal aroma of a Basil, or **Ocimum** leaf, and have been known to cross the road to escape the overwhelming scent of **Tilia**, the Linden tree in bloom. **Daphne** is both the common and botanical name for a shade-loving, evergreen shrub with a spicy fragrance. Hortense derives from Hortensia, a popular folk name for **Hydrangea**. **Hyacinth**, like Daphne has no common name, but packs the most punch when it comes to perfume. Every name was originally made up by someone. People often change their names, and plant names get changed, too. Above all, we hope that life will be sweet for the tiny flowers in our care, whatever we decide to call them or who they grow up to be!

pot peeve

pot.

the simple, iconic, clay vessel, into which one pots a potted plant.

potter.

the person who makes the pot, through the magic of the potter's wheel, in a pottery studio. no plants are potted in the potter.

potty.

the commode, or privy, the 'pot', for short. Formed of glazed ceramic, much like pottery. Occasionally seen potted with plants.

Chapter Three

101½ Ways to Enjoy Plants

It's So Easy Being Green

A BEAN GROWS IN BROOKLYN

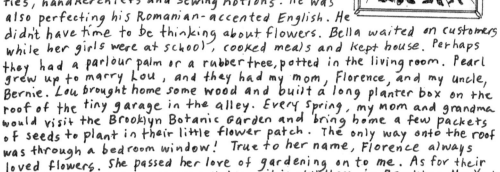

Three generations of my family lived in their apartment on St. Marks and Franklin Avenues, above my great-grandparent's corner store. The building was just completed in 1920 when Julius Berkowitz shut his shop on the Lower East Side and moved into this shiny, new "house" with his wife, Bella, and their two girls, Pearl and Rose. Julius was busy keeping his counters stocked with starched shirt collars, neckties, handkerchiefs and sewing notions. He was also perfecting his Romanian-accented English. He didn't have time to be thinking about flowers. Bella waited on customers while her girls were at school, cooked meals and kept house. Perhaps they had a parlour palm or a rubber tree, potted in the living room. Pearl grew up to marry Lou, and they had my mom, Florence, and my uncle, Bernie. Lou brought home some wood and built a long planter box on the roof of the tiny garage in the alley. Every spring, my mom and grandma would visit the Brooklyn Botanic Garden and bring home a few packets of seeds to plant in their little flower patch. The only way onto the roof was through a bedroom window! True to her name, Florence always loved flowers. She passed her love of gardening on to me. As for their "house" — that's what we always called it — it is still there, in Brooklyn, New York.

In more recent times, the storefront has been home to a Bodega, an upscale Bistro called, The Lazy Ibis, and currently, Bicycle Roots. So, bikes also grow in Brooklyn.

what's GREEN on the INSIDE?
or, does house + plant = houseplant?

A CAPTIVE AUDIENCE

Just as pets and zoo animals depend on humans to provide them with water, food and care, a plant living in a pot can't seek its own resources. Its roots can't reach down into the window sill to find a drink. It can't raise the blinds to see the sun. It is up to you and me, its trusty housemates, to make sure it has the basic enrichment it requires.

Houseplants are friends, not food.

SPIKE

JUNIOR

PUTTING THE DOOR IN INDOORS

Apart from those plants thriving on the ocean floor — which is still, technically out-of-doors, there are virtually zero plants that originate indoors in nature. Every "indoor" plant grows outdoors in some corner of the world, usually in a considerably larger size. Who brought the first plant indoors? Who invented the first door? Who's coming to dinner, because this guy is cooking! I even think he's shaved!

UG

NOT FROM AROUND HERE

The majority of plants we pot indoors year-round are from tropical places. Plants which are native to temperate zones — where winters are cold — do not make good houseplants. That is because they either go dormant, drop their leaves and look boring, or their lifespans are cut short. The only true natives in my house are these two mischievous cats, who were born on the porch.

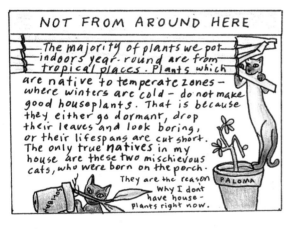

PALOMA

They are the reason why I don't have houseplants right now.

UP, POT, UP!

Plants don't pot themselves, you know. We have to do it for them. In much the same way as our cats seem to outgrow their favorite toy of the month or paté flavor — but, thankfully, less often — our houseplants will outgrow their pots. A goldfish can stay small until you provide it with a larger bowl, but a plant whose roots have crowded out the soil will start to decline if you don't up-pot it to a slightly larger container after a few years.

DRACO

OUTSIDE-INSIDE-OUT

Some people like to treat their houseplants to a summer vacation by putting them outside for the warmer months. Here are some cautions, if you are considering the idea. Sunlight, even filtered through glass, can burn leaves, and direct sun is stronger, so set your tender babies in partial shade. Make sure you remember to water them, even if you're on vacation! When you bring them back in — well before the first frost — check the leaves and soil for any bugs who may have moved in...

...It is easier to spray insects out in the yard or garage than it is to eradicate them once you've let them into the house. Plus, bug spray stinks!

NOW TRENDING

Like hairstyles, houseplant varieties go in and out of fashion. In the 1970's you had to have a Swedish Ivy. It wasn't Swedish and it wasn't Ivy, but everybody had one! There's always been some version of a potted fig, or Ficus, and the recent favorite has been F. lyrata, the Fiddle-leaf fig. It's tidier than F. benjamina, which would shed a half-dozen leaves every time you looked at it. The prince of figs, though, has to be F. elastica, the Rubber Tree Plant. A song, called "High Hopes" tells about it.

Okay, the song was really more about some crazy, optimistic ant who tries to move a Rubber Tree Plant. We all know there is never only one ant, so the question, "oh yeah? You and what army are gonna move that Rubber Tree Plant??" answers itself.

Let us now present this year's
O.U.C.H.
A W A R D S
for Outstanding Unhuggability in a Cactus-like Houseplant

Welcome to our gala event! Let me begin by saying that one **cactus** plus another **cactus** equals two **cacti** — never two **cactuses** or three **cactuses** — just a prickly point I needed to get out of the way. Not all cacti are prickly, and not all prickly plants are cacti. Not all of our award winners tonight are prickly or cacti, but you've got to give them all points for punctuality and picant personality. Now that I've taken a few pokes at a pet peeve, I shall introduce some of our favorites: please applaud all of our popular potted performers. If you can't resist high-fives and handshakes, there are tweezers available in the Lobby.

The Worst-Dressed AWARD

what they're wearing:

goes to F. grusonii, a "Barrel Cactus". In Latin, his genus, Ferocactus, means ferocious or savage, but he's really an easygoing fellow. His cousins, the Echinocacti, get their name from Echinos, the Greek word for Hedgehog. All are spiny, round and roly-poly. Let's roll out the barrel for this scruffy contestant!

The Best-Dressed AWARD

was captured, without question, by Mammillaria, a "Pincushion Cactus." Ever the sharp dresser, with an eye for novel accessorizing. She flowers, she fruits — and she designs her own wardrobe. Will her fashion flair catch on? We'll be watching with anticipation, as we are hooked!

Most Traditional Costume AWARD

a surprising star turn for Astrophytum miriostigma, alias "Bishop's Hat Cactus." Virtually spineless — but no less virtuous — he normally shies away from the spotlight.

Honorary Royalty AWARD

a curtsy for Rebutia, our semi-hardy "Crown Cactus." She was looking a little wobbly, so we gave her a throne. Well done, Ma'am.

Puzzling Name AWARD

we gave this one to O. tuna, a "Prickly Pear Cactus." The O stands for Opuntia, because it grew near Opuntis, in ancient Greece. Tuna is from the Mexican name for this edible "pear" — which is not actually a fruit, nor is it a fish.

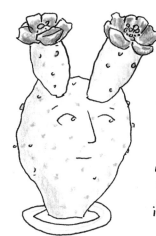

The Clear a Room AWARD

there's nothing quite like her, Stapelia grandiflora, the "Starfish Cactus." Say it with flowers, or say it with dead fish. Woo-eee — it's no way to woo!

Best Musical Performance AWARD

who else could snag this one but the "Organ-Pipe Cactus" ensemble, Stenocereus thurberi. Steno is Greek for narrow. They make up for their slenderness by sticking together, occasionally sticking one another with those short, sharp spines.

The Sheer, Stubborn Longevity AWARD

it had to be you, C. senilis, the "Old Man Cactus." Cephalocereus is also Greek, with kephale = a head cereus = a wax taper or candle. He does rather appear to be melting under the stage lighting. His wispy white hair makes him look old, whence the name senilis.

Oh, me a chin' spines!

Just Too Cute AWARD

I know, I know. It goes to one of these silly things every year, but give it up, anyway for the "Moon Cactus," or "Cactus Bunny," even if you know she's had work done... Every one of these brightly colored show stoppers is a Gymnocalycium grafted atop a Hylocerus. Who cares. They're adorable.

You Coulda Fooled Me AWARD

Euphorbia trigona: it's angular, fleshy, sappy, drought-tolerant, and also armed with some nasty spikes. But the "Crown of Thorns" is not a cactus, and along with its many prickly and caustic cousins, has a reputation for rivaling the most ferocious of Ferocacti. Beware!

Special Mentions

Best Makeup, to Mammillaria bocasana, the "Powder Puff Cactus."

Best Bone Structure, to Acanthocereus tetragonus, the multi-tiered "Fairy Castle Cactus."

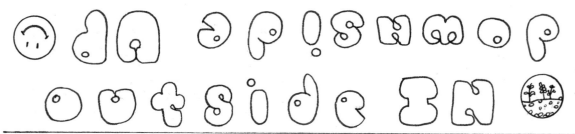

Glass is created in nature when rock and sand are heated to extreme temperatures during a volcanic eruption or lightning strike. It took until about 3000 B.C. for people to figure out how to make a big enough, hot enough furnace to melt a significant quantity of silica to produce useful glass objects. We use glass in so many different everyday ways that it's difficult to imagine that for thousands of years no one saw their own likeness in a mirror — a looking-glass — poured a beverage from a transparent bottle, looked out at the view through a plate-glass window or closed a window against the wind. Glass panes keep the rain out while letting the light in. We have come a long way from drafty castles with narrow slits in their thick stone walls to houses made almost entirely of glass. Most people don't live in glass houses, which don't afford much privacy and can get incredibly hot in summer. Plants, on the other hand thrive inside special glass houses which we call greenhouses.

The frame of a backyard, or 'hobby' greenhouse can be of metal or wood. Old, assorted window frames make a fun, eclectic hothouse. Pre-fab kits typically include translucent polycarbonate panels, which are lightweight, slightly frosted and unbreakable. This one includes an automatic vent panel, to let some of the heat escape. There is a wax-filled hinge that raises the panel when the wax begins to soften. A hobby greenhouse is a great place to jump-start vegetable and bedding plants while it is still too chilly to plant them in the garden. Some people use them to display orchids and other tropical plant collections, adding a safe heater for winter. My little poly-pocket house protects seedling trees and starts made from rooted cuttings, all waiting to become part of my miniature bonsai forest, someday soon.

A terrarium is an environment under glass, but one that is small enough to live indoors, on a table or windowsill. You can use a glass jar, goldfish bowl or aquarium. Add pebbles to the bottom, and water sparingly, because there is no drainhole. You can see the soil through the glass. A desert-scape needs no lid, while a mini jungle is happy in a mason jar.

You can make it fun by adding tiny toy people or animals, such as little plastic dinosaurs.

Tom Greenthumb

Once there was a little man
with tiny feet and tiny hands.
He made a little garden plan.
His garden space was very small.
It hadn't any room at all.
Yet, he grew a big tree only
inches tall!

BON·SAI

In the movie, *The Karate Kid*, Mr. Miyagi tends his bonsai garden everyday. It is one of his metaphors for discipline.

in literal translation means **tree** grown in a **pot**. That oversimplifies the traditional technique of training a tree to appear like its counterpart in nature while keeping it miniaturized. Bonsai trays are shallow pots with little space for roots to grow, which produces an intriguing display of twisting roots at the surface. The practice began in **China** during the Han Dynasty, over two thousand years ago. The Chinese name is **Penjing**.

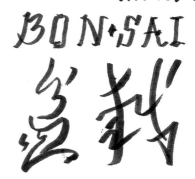

Bonsai need regular root and branch pruning. Tools are small to match the size of the trees. Wire is used to bend branches dramatically. The soil mix is lean and rocky. Moss adds a final touch on top.

There are often two drainage holes. A wire fed into one and out the other can anchor the tree roots to hold it upright.

There are many styles and choices of plant species.

The emperor wanted to be able to look out of his palace window and see his entire empire, so his gardeners made a living diorama. They represented landscapes from various locales, all in miniature, using pots. The art was embraced enthusiastically in **Japan**.

the Forcing Issue

"Fall" flowerbulbs bloom in spring. "Spring" flowerbulbs bloom in summer or fall. Their designated "names" refer to the season in which we plant them outdoors, and yes, it does sound like opposite-speak. Why not simply plant fall bulbs in the autumn and spring bulbs in the spring and summer bulbs in summer? Well, you can do that with potted bulbs which are already in bloom at any one of those seasons, but if you wish to plant lots of them, it is less expensive to buy a package of onion-like, dormant bulbs, and put them in the soil off-season.

Fall

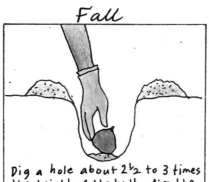

Dig a hole about 2½ to 3 times the height of the bulb. Aim the growing point upwards. You can mix a bit of bulb food in with the soil you put back.

Winter

The bulb hides under the soil — even under snow — putting down some roots. You won't see it — unless a squirrel digs it up...

Spring

It has sprouted leaves and a beautiful flower. This is what you waited months to see!

Summer

The flower is gone, but the leaves continue to feed the bulb. A baby bulb or two grow.

This is the relaxing life cycle of the "Fall" bulb.

When 'tis the season to be freezin' and we long for a little garden cheer, we wake up those normally dormant flower bulbs. and get them to bloom for us indoors.

OH COME ALL YE FAITHFUL HARK! THE HERALD ANGELS SING DECK THE HALLS WITH BOUGHS OF HOLLY FA LA LA LA LA JUST HEAR THOSE SLEIGH BELLS JINGLING RING TING TINGALING SLEEP IN HEAVENLY PEACE

They must be tricked into thinking that winter has passed and it is now time to bloom. Someone discovered that the "Paperwhite" Narcissus and the Hyacinth share both a potent fragrance and a particularly gullible nature, so they became the traditional subjects for **forcing**. First, the bulbs must be **chilled**, to simulate a brief winter. Then they are gently blasted awake by the sounds of angelic holiday music. Do not feed them fruitcake, no matter how strongly you are tempted to discard your slice in a potted plant. Your bulbs will be making only a brief, but showy appearance, and will not require any nutrients, but in order to keep them upright through the busy holiday hoopla, you will have to anchor their roots. This may be done by providing a bowl or vase with some clean pebbles or marbles at the bottom. Fill this vessel with water up to the top of the pebble line, and set your bulb on top. The idea is to keep the bulb from falling in while it sends its roots downward. There are specialized forcing vases, too, but any glass or bowl will do the job.

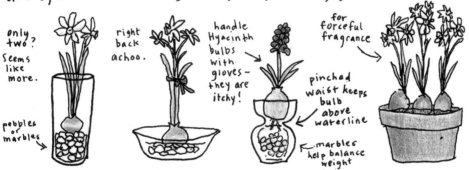

only two? Seems like more.

pebbles or marbles →

right back achoo.

handle Hyacinth bulbs with gloves - they are itchy!

for forceful fragrance

pinched waist keeps bulb above waterline

← marbles help balance weight

It's also okay to pot them in soil. Just don't get carried away. The more do not make the merrier!

A few important things to remember:

Keep your **cats** away from the **BULBS!**

⟨toxic.⟩

Keep your **dogs** away from the **CHOCOLATE!**

⟨toxic.⟩

Leave the **cookies** for **SANTA!**

⟨nice.⟩

Re-gift the **fruitcake** to your **HOSTESS**

⟨naughty.⟩

Ask for just enough **snow** to make a tiny little **SNOWMAN.**

YES PARKING

We all need our **parks**, small and large. They provide a re-set and a respite from all of the paved surfaces and artificial structures that surround us everywhere. Parks are special, designated green spaces we set aside for public enjoyment of **nature**. For city dwellers, parks are often the only place to get some fresh air or picnic on the grass. Even dogs have their own parks these days, where they can run off-leash and have play dates with their own kind.

National Parks now cover more than thirteen million acres of the U.S. The concept of preserving the magnificent beauty of our vast, natural landscape was almost an afterthought. **Yellowstone**, in Wyoming, was declared the first national park in 1872 by an act of Congress. Twelve such parks had been established by 1916, when the National Park Service was formed to manage our growing park system. The stated purpose of that system is, " To conserve the scenery and the natural and historical objects and the wildlife therein, and to provide for the enjoyment of same in such manner and by such means as will leave them unimpaired for the enjoyment of future generations. " If not for the Yellowstone Act, millions of acres of bold and pristine wilderness would be open to private purchase, construction, destruction and commercial exploitation. Preserving wildlife habitat and clean water is even more of a reason to protect these lands than the fact that their beauty is sacred to some and enjoyed by most humans. In the twenty-first century, lands and animals are threatened by proposals and projects aiming to access fossil fuels in previously protected areas. On a smaller scale, visitors like us can do our part not to damage natural areas, and to pack out our trash.

What belongs in the PARK?

bird's nest   chip bag   mushrooms   spare tire   log bench   signs   graffiti

clear-cut trees   old hiking boot   bunny   coffee cup   snail   butt   bottle

In 1938, a New York City developer introduced a plan to integrate greenscape and multi-family housing. The community of **Parkchester** was designed and built in the Bronx. The layout, which had a series of detached brick apartment buildings surrounding green plazas, was a novel break from traditional urban residential patterns. The usual sight in a metropolitan neighborhood is a long block of uninterrupted, attached tall buildings with windows on the front and back walls, many with storefronts at street level. Nervous trees might emerge near the curb through a hole in the sidewalk, their trunks caged in iron to protect them from traffic.

40,000 people call Parkchester home!

When my grandma's sister Rose married Sidney, they moved into one of the new buildings at Parkchester, where they raised my cousins, Jane and Joe. Throughout my childhood, it was to Aunt Rose's park-like apartment we would go, for every Thanksgiving dinner. Parkchester is still a happy neighborhood.

Old Westbury Gardens followed the tradition of turning a formerly private estate grounds and residence into a park for group visits and events. We piled into school buses for countless class trips and Girl Scout maypole pageants, politely stepping among the roses and perfect lawns, and always keeping a lookout for the resident peacock. A peanut butter sandwich tastes special in a park.

Best pay toll to the peacock.

Jones Beach State Park was where we all flocked to in the summertime. Mom would pack us all into the car — kids plus friends, blanket, umbrella, towels, buckets, picnic lunch — and off we'd go to spend the day digging holes, building castles, collecting shells and chasing the breaking tides. There are not many trees at the beach, and the plant life is mainly grasses, reeds and seaweed, but the **state park** designation protects the land from commercial development, preserving access for the public's recreation and ensuring maintenance.

Cindy's Sequoia is an amazing Giant Redwood, growing across the alley that separates our houses. About twenty-two years ago, my neighbor, Cindy took her son, Taylor to California to visit the Redwood Forest, a park with trees so large you can drive a car through some of their trunks. They purchased a tiny seedling tree as a souvenir, and planted it in their backyard. At least for now, they are still driving around the trunk.

You can **hug** a sequoia with the help of your friends.

TURNING GREEN...

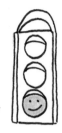

but in a good way.

IF you are really into plants, then you may be interested in a future career in what is known as the **Green Industry.** Botanists are horticultural scientists who have completed university degrees to learn the microscopic secrets of how plants grow. There is much to learn about plants, but there are other green avenues that don't require as many years of formal study, and you can gain tremendous knowledge as you work around other "plant people."

Horticultural scientists are **plant** biologists, for the most part, but the plant world is inseparable from the insect world, and insects are plant-loving animals. Bugs don't chew holes in plants to be destructive, but to eat or create shelter. **Agrichemists** work in labs testing pesticides which will be used by farmers to protect our food crops. The hopeful trend for the 21st century is our continual movement away from poisonous chemicals, which end up in rivers and streams and the wildlife inhabitants of those environments. Using earth-friendly pest controls is another way of turning green! If you enjoyed the test-tubey, microscopey activities in your lab science classes, but not so much the dissecty, gutsy parts, then a plant science career may appeal to you. **Botanists** study what plants look like and how they grow, naming and grouping them according to the similarities in their flowers and cones. Some botanists are **Geneticists,** enhancing certain characteristics of existing plants, making crosses between species, which is called **hybridization** and results in new, man-made **cultivars.** Plant improvements can increase crop yields and pest resistance.

Plant collectors lead exciting lives of travel, heading all over the globe to photograph, catalogue and accumulate samples of unusual species. An ethical collector knows to get permission to remove samples, transport plant matter across borders and **never** take every example of a species from its home.

Seed Savers perform a critical function for us all, by maintaining a protected, temperature-controlled library of seeds of all kinds. Plants, like animals can become extinct. Diversity not only makes the world more interesting. It also reduces the danger of species starvation and famine caused by an insect or disease blight wiping out a monocrop. Seeds guarantee future plant life!

Growers operate commercial **Nurseries** of varying sizes. They maintain tree farms and greenhouses filled with plant starts of all types — edible and ornamental — most of the growing stock that eventually ends up in our gardens.

Wholesale nurseries do most of the growing, and don't tend to be open to the general public, but they do sell large quantities of plants directly to landscapers. Staff at a growing operation plant seeds by the thousands into trays and flats and pony-packs. They water, fertilize and watch for bugs and diseases like mildew as the seedlings grow. They also start new plants as cuttings from mature parent stock — cuttings that have put out **adventitious roots**.

Tagging and labeling rows and rows of pots and trays helps ensure that the plant turns out to be what the customer believes they are buying. Seedlings can look remarkably similar! There are not too many gardeners who enjoy the surprise of having their "pink" begonias turn out to be white and big landscapes have to match.

Rooted tree cuttings grow in deep plastic cups, in special soil-less medium, to keep the moisture level just right. Once roots have formed a solid **plug**, each tree gets its own larger pot, usually undergoing a series of up-potting events until it is big enough to be sold.

Boo-Bear Posie

A bar-code on the back of the tag is scanned-ready at the counter

A **hoop house** is another style of greenhouse made of plastic stretched over bowed tubes. It is often seen at grower facilities. Rails along the ceiling support hanging flower baskets, which are a popular item for patios. They need lots of space to be big enough by spring.

Retail nurseries and **Garden Centers** purchase the wholesale growers' products and display them attractively for us to buy. In addition to a wide range of plant material, a good retail nursery will be well stocked with tools, pottery, soil, fertilizers, gloves, seeds, watering cans, gardening books and knowledgeable staff.

Garden Designers can help you make the best use of your available space and help you decide on the right plants for shade versus sun and high-versus low maintenance requirements. They will visit your yard, discuss your likes and dislikes, and give you a plan. They can usually recommend a reliable landscaper, should you need planting help, or if you desire **hardscape** decks, paving or terracing — point you to a **Landscape Architect**, **stone** patio expert or perhaps a **carpenter**.

Arborists know about tree health and proper pruning. A certified expert loves trees and will provide the best care and advice.

Landscapers work outdoors in all weather, planting, trimming, weeding and mulching. A good landscaper will have enough plant expertise to distinguish a weed from your beloved **specimen**!

DON'T CAST AWAY YOUR LIVERWORTS

Chapter Four

The Emerald Kingdom

Growing Underfoot
and Overhead

the lowly
moss club

Moss does exactly grow on trees, you know! It also grows quite happily on roofing shingles, rocks, and shaded pavement. That tells us that the moss is not a **parasite** ~ it is not sapping any nutrients from the tree bark ~ as not even moss can squeeze blood from a stone. Moss, a quite ancient and primitive life form, is to be admired for its ability to subsist upon the barest amount of moisture, absorbed directly through its tissues, going dormant when no moisture is available. Seekers of the perfect lawn fight back the gentle moss, as it hunkers down in the shadows of the blades of grass, but moss asks so little of the gardener, no mowing or feeding.

How can you join the Lowly Moss Club? There are a few rules establishing what it takes to qualify as a **true** moss, but these kids are pretty easygoing, low-maintenance types, so they'll let you come and visit at the very least.

True mosses are **Bryophytes**. They contain green chlorophyll, which they use to convert sunlight into energy, thereby qualifying as plants, but they have no roots, leaves or stems, and they don't reproduce by seed. They make more moss by releasing tiny, dust-like spores from capsules borne atop spindly threads. They have no vascular system ~ the 'veins' higher plants use to move water up and food down through their tissues ~ and they lack a waxy cuticle, or skin to seal moisture inside. One evolutionary step up from these simple sorts are the **Lycopodophytes**, which we call **club** mosses. These guys *do* have stems, leaves and pipelines, and a clubhouse of their own. They consider themselves superior to the true, lowly mosses, which, technically speaking they are, but only in complexity. Club mosses still produce spore, not seed, and do not flower, either. But every moss is cute, soft, spongy, low-growing, and intricate ~ up close!

(Signs on clubhouse:) Leaves keep out! / NO roots allowed / low clearance / Keep cool / No cuticles! / No stems or veins

Seta = stalk, bearing an immature capsule

ripe capsule

sporophyte = spore-producing body

gametophyte colony = dozens of tiny, green plants

spore, actual size

and in an enlarged micrograph

There are different species of moss, and some of them resemble tiny ferns, or Jack Frost, in green. I have collected several kinds in my forest terrarium, home to an indoor lowly moss club, all thriving inside a glass cookie jar.

You can pull up a little moss mat and take it home in your pocket, where it will go brown, should you forget it, but revive and green up again in a jar with a bit of damp soil. (I don't think a trip through the washer and dryer would do it much good, so try not to forget it for that long!) My jar has been stuck shut for years ~ still green!

a Frond, indeed

A fern is another prehistoric plant form, larger than a moss, and possessing stems, roots and leaves, like all of the woody or leafy garden plants, but still producing spores rather than seeds, and so, lacking flowers. As plain as that makes them sound, ferns are sought-after ornamentals, thriving in the garden's deepest shade. Some species have been admired as house plants for centuries, as well.

We call each leaf a **frond**; and each new frond emerges from the center of the plant's base as a tightly curled spiral. As with mosses, the frond is a spore-producing **sporophyte**, springing from a base called a **gametophyte**. Fern spores can germinate new plants in the cracks along a tree's bark, or in the crevices along a rock wall, producing such lush sights as a hanging fern grotto ~ a seemingly living cliff or cave. Let's take a look at a fern's two life stages.

STAGE ONE: (it's kind of chicken and egg, really.) The mature sporophyte develops **sporangia**, which appear as brown, fuzzy dots in neat rows along the leaf's underside.

STAGE TWO: (from the chicken's point of view.) The spores ripen and burst free from their capsules. They must find a moist place to land and germinate. If they succeed, and sprout a living, green island-like platform, there is how a **gameto-phyte**. This strange little island contains **antheridium cells** (male) and **archegonium cells** (female) on its underside, which must combine their **gametes** to make a new **sporophyte**.

A fully-opened frond

A frond that has yet to unfurl is called a fiddle-head (looks like the top of a violin) or a crozier (also looks like a shepherd's crook). Some immature fronds are cooked and eaten, but don't try this with any random fern you find. You can buy them at the grocery store, if you'd like to try some.

A magnified spore finds water and germinates into a **prothallus** which grows to form a gametophyte.

boys — rhizoid root starts — girls

The gametophyte will shrivel and turn brown.

This is the primary leaf, a new, baby sporophyte

Incidentally — not all fern fronds look like this: ! There are also ferns that look like this, this, and this.

covering some ground

Soil, earth...dirt, is the foundation of the plant world, but it's not particularly interesting to look at. While it's important to leave a little space on the ground between the trees, shrubs and bedding plants, not all of that 'empty' real estate will be pathways or patio. Spreading play chips or bark mulch is one way to keep the dust down — and prevent mud, when that dust gets wet — but there is another way to hide the bare soil. Meet... the **ground covers**.

Creepers grow very low to the ground, so you can step over them — or, in most cases, on them, even if it seems a little mean. Some of them give off a delicious scent when trodden underfoot, and they'll spring right back up.

Penstemon barrettii, another easy, shade-loving evergreen bloomer.

Vinca, or periwinkle, is a hardy evergreen. Kind of a classic, it thrives in the shade.

Fragaria chiloensis, Beach strawberry. Drought-tolerant, deep evergreen, grows anywhere, asking nothing of you. Tiny berries.

Lonicera crassifolia, or cress-leaved honey-suckle. Also evergreen. Not edible, but cute.

Thymus, thyme, even the one used in cooking. There are some very low, tight knit varieties, my favorite being Elfin thyme.

Teuchrium, germander. All varieties are hardy. They grow while you watch.

Geranium macrorrhizum the bigroot geranium, is a broad-leaved, scented, blooming cranesbill I use everywhere.

Helianthemum, or sun rose. Multiple leaf and flower colors. Fabulous evergreen.

Subshrubs will fill out an area to create a green understory or help prevent slope erosion. They are generally too tall or woody to step on. Many of them multiply via seed or root sucker, forming a spreading colony. They will out-compete dainty bedding plants, so you should place them away from small ornamentals.

Genista is a broom with arched, mounding branches. Smaller than a Scotch broom, but related and equally hardy.

Lavandula, lavender. So many to choose from. Why stop at just one? Sachets!!

Rosmarinus, yes, Rosemary, but look for creeping cultivars, such as 'Irene', which simply drips beauty.

Ceanothus griseus horizontalis, Carmel creeper, will remain horizontal if you don't train it up a chainlink fence!

Vine by the Yard

Could someone remind me why I planted so many vines? most have interesting leaves or pretty, sweet-smelling flowers. Some have fruit that isn't grapes. Vines stop growing during the winter months, but when spring comes they are off to the races, so get ready (but don't run with clippers).

Others cling to walls with sticky rootlets or suction cups! Some vines would wind around you overnight, if you stood perfectly still, asleep on your feet. Vines are wonderful (not strangling the nearest tree), its fruit doesn't make a mess on the ground, or germinate a hundred seedlings.

Never believe anyone who tells you something that is not chocolate tastes like chocolate, which the bizarre, messy fruit of the "Chocolate Vine" clearly does not.

but astonishing for its seemingly infinite length. Vines require regular pruning and training, usually, and you don't have to be shy about chopping as it only makes them stronger.

A vine is not compact or shrubby, but astonishing for its seemingly infinite length. As with trees, there is no vine family, and also why the previous owner of this house...

Honeysuckle vines need taming, usually along some type of rigid trellis, fence or arbor. Vining is more of a habit, or the growing style of a plant.

Sigh. I know why people love it, even though there are countless other vines from which grapes do not grow.

It grows several inches per day. It grows before your very eyes! It climbs up into the orchard where hundreds of grape vines are planted. Grapes are known as 'fruit of the vine,' but what a beauty! The yard is an orchard.

A vine is... A beauty!

Holboellia (China Blue Vine) is my new favorite evergreen vine. Some stays evergreen, most...

Lonicera (Honeysuckle) smells great, with L. halliana offering the best fragrance. Some, by their main stem, and some by their leaf stalks.

Wisteria

Akebia (Chocolate Vine) is nearly evergreen. ...fill up your compost bin with slimy, alien brain pods.

when is a "PINE" not a "PINE?"

It's roughly triangular in shape, like a trademark Xmas tree. Its leaves are needles. It smells... *clean*. It stays green all year. Nothing much seems to grow beneath it. It *must* be a **Pine**! Unless, of course, it is a **Fir**, or a **Spruce**, or a **Hemlock**, or a true **Cedar** (or a **False Hemlock**). Don't give up hope of telling them apart. All of these distinguished trees are members of **Pinaceae**, the Pine Family. With their fragrant, needle-shaped leaves and radiating, tiered branches, many people simply lump them together and call them all pines. Here are some tips to help you distinguish one giant from another.

All **pines** belong to the Latin genus, **Pinus**. There are lots of pine species, but all drop oodles of old, golden-brown leaves each year. These grow in bundles called **fascicles**, with either two, three or five needles stuck together. Pine needles can be deep green or almost blue, with a white stripe, but all are at least 1½ to 2 inches long. Pine bark can be smooth and grey to brown, but it isn't peely. The fruit is a woody cone, which varies from about 2 inches all the way up to 7 or so, in the mighty Ponderosa pine. A dried, ripe cone pops open to reveal its seeds, which usually have a small wing to help them travel on the breeze. Some pine 'nuts' are delicious. (do you eat pesto?)

UNRIPE   DRIED   ACTUAL SIZE OF A PINE NUT (plural: pignioli)

True cedars are **Cedrus**. Ten or more needles, short and sharp (!) make up each bundle. Their cones are chubby and barrel-shaped, standing upright along the branches. When ripe, they shatter into individual seeds, leaving a bare spindle.

Every fir is **Abies**, and has flattened, short, individual needles. When the needles occasionally drop, they leave little pockmarks on the wood. Their cones are smaller than cedar cones, but also sit upright and shatter to spread their seeds.

A spruce looks an awful lot like a fir, but its genus is **Picea**. The trick to spruce I.D. is the little pegs left on the stems after needle drop. A spruce cone stays intact, like a pinecone, and dangles, long and curvy.

Hemlocks are **Tsuga**, and sport tiny, adorable cones and short, randomly-angled individual needles. I ♡ them.

Pseudotsuga literally means "False Hemlock", but we call them Douglas Fir, just to keep everybody guessing. Their cones are a useful clue, as you will hear.

Cone-y Island Treasure

raaa!

Todo lo que brilla no es oro!

A fine, pine chest, of course! 'Twas me Granny's.

Arrrr, 'tis a treasure, to be sure, and they're mine, all mine! But if ye come close enough to look me in the eye, I may tell ye where ta find a few cones o' yer own. Only, don't be too quick ta be callin' em *pine* cones. Some is impostors! Mind me words — not me grammar — do a bit o' studyin' up, and keep yer slimy hooks off me bounty, gents! I plan on stringin' meself a pretty garland or two, and one fer me Polly, here, who's got 'er "aaarrrrs" backwards, but she's a fine old cone-picker, to be sure!

Picea
Spruce cones dangle downward, tantalizingly. The scales are thin and slightly curved, like me fingernails ~ which I've stopped biting. Been workin' on me hygiene, see. Never know who ye might meet once ashore...

Pinus
If 'tis a sturdy cone yer after, ye'll not do better than to pick up a woody pine cone. They vary a-plenty in size, but pines is pines, as sure as eggs is eggs.

Tsuga
Were ye wantin' some fine, tiny cones, fer makin' a friendship bracelet, say, which — mind yer assumptions ~ I have been known to do, from time to time, then hemlock's yer choice. Kin fit a dozen or more in me watch pocket.

Larix
Happen ye finds some precious wee cones one fine winter day, only there's barely a needle on the branch. What ye'll have before ye is a larch ~ a deciduous conifer! Come spring, it'll look just like a cedar.

Pseudotsuga
A puzzler, indeed, when it comes ta names, but an easier cone is not to be had. Ye'll know a Doug fir by the little mousies trapped under every scale, tryin' ta hide.

Abies 'n' Cedrus
No chance o' findin' a fir or cedar cone off the tree, unless it be the work of some sorcery. Scaly seeds is all there'll be, so take a nice snapshot er two, fer the album, like.

TREES of LIFE

I shall now sing ~ or, perhaps write ~ of the virtues of trees. Trees are majestic ~ impressive in their size and age. Some species of tree can live for more than one hundred years. During their lifetimes, they perform several valuable, even invaluable services for the planet. They provide us with food, in the form of fruit, nuts and leaves. Sundry items can be obtained from various parts. Cork is harvested from the bark of the cork oak, *Quercus suber*, in great sheets, without harming the tree.

APPLE

ALMOND

KAFFIR LIME

ASPIRIN

Salix, the willow, has **salicylic acid** in its bark. You may recognize that as the pain-relieving substance in aspirin, and Native Americans benefited from willow bark long before there was such a thing as a pill, capsule or tablet. Chewing on twigs, especially **Peelu**, will clean your teeth. Taxol, derived from the toxic berry of **Taxus**, the yew tree, was an early cancer treatment drug.

Shade from tree canopies cools not only us but the Earth. Tree roots anchor soil in place, controlling erosion and preventing landslides. Farmland out on the endless flat prairies becomes a dust bowl, without occasional **shelterbelts** of trees and shrubs to break the fierce winds. Trees absorb carbon dioxide and pollutants.

Trees come in many beautiful shapes:

Pyramidal

columnar

broadly spreading

weeping

windswept

Trees produce color and fragrance with their leaves, bark, oils and flowers

cinnamon bark

cedar sachet

Trees provide homes for many animal species

beavers

monkeys
squirrels
lemurs

birds
people

Living trees are the most valuable asset our planet has to offer us, after drinkable water, but dead trees also have a worthy afterlife. Once they have fallen naturally, they begin to decompose, hollowing out inside and becoming hosts to small creatures, insects

and fungi (mushrooms thrive on rotting logs). Often, a seed dropped from above will land in one of these logs and start a new tree. For many centuries, most trees that have fallen have been **felled**, by fellers known as **fallers**, **loggers** and **lumberjacks**. These are

A nurse log

people who work in the **timber** industry. Lumber, timber or simply, **wood** is what a tree becomes when it is no longer attached to its roots, and people all over the world have found ways to make use of wood.

Wood grain is what we call the swirling patterns in a cut piece of wood

From simple branch and twig huts to elaborate framework, most of our dwellings are made of wood, as are most of our fences and furniture. Mill wheels and wagon wheels were wooden, and when horse-drawn carriages began to be replaced by the 'horse-less carriage' — that's what early automobiles were called — cars were largely constructed out of wood! Wood is strong, and unlike metal and stone, it is a **renewable** resource. As long as new seedlings are planted as old trees are harvested for lumber, fuel, paper and furniture, the planet will never run out of wood. We have figured out how to '**save a tree**' by recycling used paper into new paper and cardboard. Sawdust and odd scraps that are lumber mill leftovers get pressed and glued together to make homely but useful, sturdy plywood sheets and boards.

Strandboard or particle board or chip board

Timber bamboo produces stalks that are as strong as tree wood, although it is a giant grass. By slicing, steaming and pressing the bamboo canes flat, they can be glued together into beautiful sheets for flooring, furniture and fencing. A ladder or scaffold made of bamboo is reliable.

Like many other industries, logging was once unregulated. Lumbering was the first industry in the American colonies, and the forests and mountainsides were so thick with trees it seemed an endless supply. As pioneers pushed westward into the frontier — in their wooden-wheeled, wooden wagons — they began to clear entire forests with no thought of conservation. Europe was happy to trade with these settlers for bountiful white pine logs which they used for wall paneling and trim, and on ships.

Can't see de **forest** for **deforestation**?
This is the scarred remains of clear-cutting.

More trees were cut to make way for roads, railways and farming. We have come a long way in our understanding and respect for our trees and forests. We recognize that we need our trees and they need us. The latest thing we are learning is that trees communicate amongst themselves via an underground network. Amazing!

23 Trees and Me

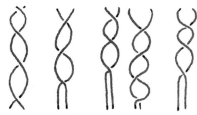

In a garden where not a single tree stood, there is now a small forest of twenty-three trees, and no two alike. That is what can happen when a tree person buys a home with an empty, neglected yard. It also helps to work for more than twenty years at a nursery with an amazing selection of trees and a great employee discount. Nevertheless, it isn't every nursery person who decides to reforest a city lot, and it took a considerable amount of digging, pruning* and planning to make sure each of these trees would have the space it needs to grow, and people would still be able to navigate a path from the street to my doorstep. The secret is to know the mature size and shape of each tree, and to stagger the placement of every one, creating an **overstory** and **understory**. The shorter trees tuck in below the branches of the taller trees, and everything fits in like pieces of a puzzle. Trees that need some shade get a bit of protection overhead, and each tree's canopy touches another's without growing through it, creating a beautiful green arbor, if you look upward. The densely shaded ground, mulched by fallen leaves, is moist and free of weeds. No raking, no mowing, and less watering.

Cotinus

Franklinia

Sciadopitys

Cornus

Stewartia

Oemleria

Betula

*no trees were **tipped** or **topped** in this garden. (see chapter six.)

So, how does a tree person choose from so many possible species and limit herself to only 23? Even with artful underplanting there is a finite amount of space. Many selections were based on trees I came to love in our school arboretum at Lake Washington. Others I had seen around the neighborhood, remembered from childhood or met at the nursery.

1. Stewartia pseudocamellia: Japanese Stewartia. The first tree to go in the ground. Amazing fall color, peeling, mosaic-like bark and zig-zag branch pattern. I had to have one.

2. Cornus capitata: an evergreen Dogwood, which is quite unusual. Acquired as a seedling from a retired ferry captain. The flowers go from cream, to pink to deep rose. Year-round beauty.

3. Oemleria cerasiformis: Indian Plum. When bare, it looks like a twin to #4, but this one has a tiny, almost daisy-like flower in deep pink or white. (mine is white.)

4. Franklinia alatamaha: Franklin Tree, named by a friend of Benjamin's after it was discovered in the wild in Georgia. Delicate branching and sweet little cupped, white flowers in mid autumn.

5. Sciadopitys verticillata: sometimes called Japanese umbrella Pine, though it's more closely related to a Sequoia. Slow growing, neat pyramid with soft, rubbery needles, red bark and cute little cones.

6. Manglietia insignis: Red Lotus. A magnolia cousin, dainty like it's other relative, Michelia but with a deep pink flower. The blossoms stand upright on the branch tips.

7. Betula jacquemontii: Himalayan White Birch. A seedling sprouted in the yard and refused to leave, so I bent it over in half and it kept growing as a weeping tree.

8. Pyrus communis: Common Pear, with three grafted fruit cultivars. Trained as a two-dimensional espalier onto a chain-link fence, which masks the homely fence while supporting the fruit.

9. Cotinus obovatus: Smoke Tree. Another great source of fall color. The flower cluster is a tumbleweed of fine, pink "smoke." A sumac, its sap is...aromatic.

10. Arbutus unedo: Strawberry Madrone. Easier to keep alive than its cousin, the Madrona. Strawberry-colored fruit is pretty, messy, and also edible, if you were starving.

11. Lagerstroemia x indica: Zuni Crape Myrtle. Never blooms in Seattle quite like the ones I saw in Texas, but the bark is pretty, leaves orange-up in fall, and I had a crazy cat named Zuni.

12. Diospyros kaki: Chinese persimmon. Okay, I did plant two of these, but only because I really, really, really hope to grow some heavenly persimmon fruit!

13. Pinus ... sylvestris? Some kind of blue-needled, un-labeled pine I picked up as a bonsai start. Once out of its small pot, it grew into quite a large tree.

14. Acer shirasawanum: Autumn gold Maple. Leaves are a stunning bright green through spring and summer. This tree is extremely slow-growing, but well worth the wait.

15. Acer circinatum: Vine Maple. This one is fast-growing, and kind of a must-have, if you live in the PNW, as it is a NW native. Takes sun or shade and delivers on fall color.

16. Ginkgo biloba: Maidenhair Tree. Mine is a 'Princeton Sentry' — tall and narrow, for a Ginkgo. If you ever see me nibbling on it, I'm probably trying to recall something medicinal??

17. Pinus strobus 'Pendula': Weeping Eastern White Pine. Puts out incredibly long, sticky cones. Takes up a lot of space, but looks like a green woolly mammoth, standing guard in the garden corner.

18. Hovenia dulcis: Japanese Raisin Tree. Does this look like a raisin to anyone? This is a dried twiglet, which tastes a bit raisiny and a bit nutty, and the squirrels get them all.

19. Abies koreana 'Horstmann's Silberlocke': A special Korean Fir, whose needles have a blue-white stripe on the underside. This one was planted for my tall, sturdy Dad.

20. Heptacodium miconioides: Seven Son Flower. Great, silvery-white peeling bark and an unusual flower form. This tree grew much taller than I had expected it to. It hangs over the deck roof.

21. Fraxinus angustifolia: Narrow-leaved Ash. (Shhh — you are mommy's favorite — don't tell your siblings.) I found it, unpriced in the back area of a small nursery and made them sell it to me.

22. Oxydendrum arboreum: Sourwood Tree. Is the wood sour? I haven't tried it. Another fall color show-off, turning vermillion orange, to red to almost purple, and even in shade.

23. Acer palmatum: Freebie Japanese Maple, grown from a rescued seedling. Big enough to share with the squirrels, who routinely nibble off branches for bedding.

Gone, but not forgotten:
24: Acer capillipes
25: Ulmus camperdownii
26: Amelanchier grandiflora
27: Pistachia chinense
28: Salix nigra 'Pendula'

Tree to Be You and Me

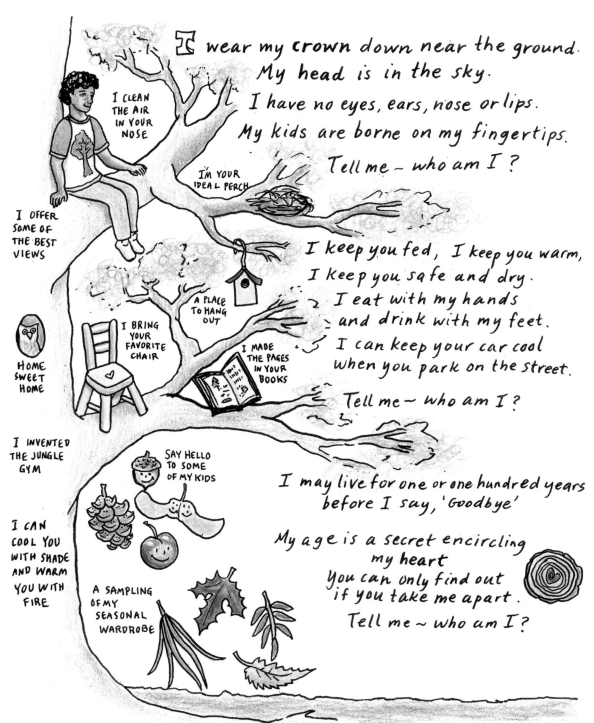

I CLEAN THE AIR IN YOUR NOSE

I OFFER SOME OF THE BEST VIEWS

I'M YOUR IDEAL PERCH

A PLACE TO HANG OUT

I BRING YOUR FAVORITE CHAIR

HOME SWEET HOME

I MADE THE PAGES IN YOUR BOOKS

I INVENTED THE JUNGLE GYM

I CAN COOL YOU WITH SHADE AND WARM YOU WITH FIRE

SAY HELLO TO SOME OF MY KIDS

A SAMPLING OF MY SEASONAL WARDROBE

I wear my crown down near the ground.
My head is in the sky.
I have no eyes, ears, nose or lips.
My kids are borne on my fingertips.
Tell me — who am I?

I keep you fed, I keep you warm,
I keep you safe and dry.
I eat with my hands
and drink with my feet.
I can keep your car cool
when you park on the street.
Tell me — who am I?

I may live for one or one hundred years
before I say, 'Goodbye'

My age is a secret encircling
my heart
You can only find out
if you take me apart.
Tell me — who am I?

You can't keep a good plant down.

There is a graceful, twenty-five foot tall Japanese maple tree in my garden. It is as pretty as any I could have bought, but this one was free. It began life as a tiny seedling that happened to sprout through a crack in an asphalt-paved parking lot. The future looked grim for that brave little sprout. Gently gripping its stem as close to the ground as possible, I pulled it up and brought it home. It spent some time in a 4" pot until it had developed enough root mass to graduate to 6" and then 8". Then I planted it in the ground, in a shady corner. It is now sufficiently large to supply the local squirrels with nesting material and still look lush. I still pluck tiny seedlings and pot them up as bonsai, because after twenty-eight years, my urban forest is full.

Angkor Wat Temple, Cambodia

This is one astonishing example of a tree planting itself and being allowed to grow in an unlikely location. The ancient Ta Prohm temple complex has undergone several restorations.

Water.
Respect it. Use it wisely,
because without water,
we would all lose our heads.

Chapter Five

Groundbreaking Science

The Outdoor Laboratory

Water babies

all of us are water babies, whether or not we like to take a bath. We spend about nine months before birth floating in a salty soup. Even the healthiest person would not last more than a week without drinkable water. There is no living thing, plant or animal, that can exist without it, although some can survive longer dry spells. Even bugs need to drink, or dine on juicy fruit — or other, juicy bugs. The average adult human takes in about one **ton** of water every year, either in beverages or in food. Seven tenths of your earthling body is water, just as about seven-tenths of Earth's surface is covered by the stuff. 1, 400, 000, 000, 000, 000, 000 tons: that is the estimated weight of all the water on the planet, and it can't seem to even out its distribution. Most of it is in the oceans, of course, but heavy rains can be flooding entire counties, while mere hours away a lack of rain is turning soil into dust. Water is constantly on the move in what we call:

The water cycle.

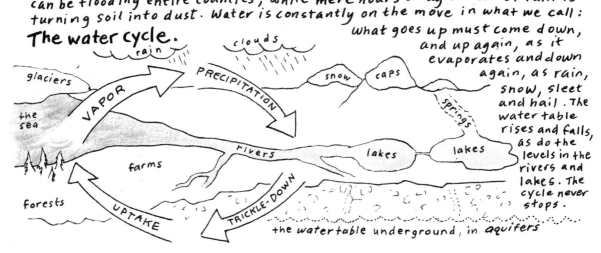

clouds
rain
glaciers
VAPOR
PRECIPITATION
the sea
snow   CAPS
springs
rivers
lakes   lakes
farms
TRICKLE-DOWN
forests
UPTAKE
the water table underground, in *aquifers*

what goes up must come down, and up again, as it evaporates and down again, as rain, snow, sleet and hail. The water table rises and falls, as do the levels in the rivers and lakes. The cycle never stops.

Rhymes with *trout*.

Droughts occur predictably and severely in some of the hottest parts of the world, drying up fields of crops. People suffer famine and herds, both domesticated and wild, turn to dry bones. At the same time as one region watches their baked soil crack, millions of others, in random places on the globe lose homes, crops, livestock and lives due to flash floods. Flooding happens when excessive amounts of rainfall occur in a brief period, bringing more water than the ground

HELP!

You can skip a bath or a swim, but fish can't — not even once. A fish out of water is an ex-fish!

can absorb or a river's banks can hold. Both droughts and floods involve water extremes. We can't prevent rainfall, but we can all do a small part in conserving our **clean water.** Turn off faucets and hoses when they're not being used.

An osmosis jones.

Jones is a slang word for a craving. Sometimes we crave a particular food — salty chip and fast-food ads on t.v. encourage those cravings — but usually we are simply hungry. When your stomach grumbles it is time to find some food, and it's not often difficult to remember to eat.

When your tongue starts to feel like a dried up sponge, you know you are thirsty and it's time to find a drink. What is your choice of beverage? Did you know that everything you drink begins with water, and that some beverages can actually make you thirstier? Some beverages contain sodium — that's **salt** — and you can taste it in tomato juice. Most kids are not big fans of tomato juice, but even the sugars and flavorings in other fruit juices and fruit "drinks" can leave you thirsty. Water is the best thing you can drink.

If your tapwater doesn't taste delicious (clean water is said to be tasteless, odorless and colorless — but most tapwater tastes to some degree of chlorine or other minerals) you can run it through a carbon filter. This does not make it fizzy (read on...) but a filter on the faucet or in a special pitcher absorbs chlorine and impurities and makes the water taste a little sweeter. I don't know exactly why, but water straight from the bathroom tap tastes great, while I can smell chlorine in the kitchen!

tap water - in a re-usable cup

Osmosis comes from the Greek word, **OSMOS**, which means a push. Water will push across a cell membrane to dilute higher concentrations of salt found within the cell. When you eat those salty chips you were jonesing for, the available water in your body will rush to put out the fire from all of that sodium. If you don't replenish your water supply, you may start to get a headache, or feel a little dizzy. If you reach for a sugary drink, especially a soda, you are adding even more substances for the water to dilute. The **soda** in soda pop is not sodium, but carbon dioxide, a gas that leaves our bodies every time we exhale.

In fizzy, carbonated drinks large amounts of the gas are compressed into liquid form. All of those bubbles are what make you burp when you drink a pop. Plants take in the carbon dioxide - CO_2 we breathe out, and couldn't live without it, but if you had no water and gave a plant some of your 8-up instead, you would quickly have a dead plant. Your plant tells you it is thirsty by doing this:

drooping leaves

curling leaves

rolling leaves

If you wait for brown or shriveling leaves, you may be too late.

The RAIN, it's PLAIN, Stays MAINLY in the DRAIN.

All plants need **water**, but how much? How often? What temperature, and what time of day? Part of your job as a successful gardener involves the science of how water behaves, in the soil as well as in — and on — a plant.

PH stands for the potential **Hydrogen** that can be measured in a liquid solution, on a scale from 0 to 14. The middle of the scale, 7, is called neutral, and as a measurement approaches ▇▇, it detects more alkalinity (a base, or basic alkaline tastes bitter). At the ▇▇ end, the solution is more **acidic**, or sour. Pure water starts out as neutral, and as other substances are dissolved into it, the neutral status moves in one direction or the other. Some plants prefer a more acidic environment, and become weak if they are transplanted to a more alkaline zone. **Rain**, which brings wonderful, free water from the sky, is essentially neutral, but it can collect acidic particles from the air on the way down.

Garden chemistry comes into play when the pH balance in the soil prevents your plants from absorbing the minerals they need to grow, thrive, bloom and produce tasty fruit.

Litmus paper test strip

1 3 5 7 9 11 13
2 4 6 8 10 12 14

Acid rain has accumulated too much **Sulfur dioxide** — air pollution — as it passed through the sky. If your plants are not growing well, you can test the **pH** of your soil with a simple chemistry set called a **pH** kit. Lime (a base) can be added to raise the alkalinity, or sulfur to lower it. Modern tapwater tends to be more alkaline than rainwater, but that only makes a noticeable difference in plants that really crave one extreme or the other, and planting soil should still be kept fairly close to the middle range.

The Caryophyllaceae Family includes a range of "Pinks" popular in old-fashioned English cottage gardens. They bloom in red, white, red + white (= pink!) and a soft yellow. The ones with large flowers are popularly known as Carnations, a prom favorite.

I'll box you!

BAKING SODA

I'll try not to bottle it!

LEMON JUICE

The Ericaceae Family includes such favorites as Erica (Heath), Calluna (Heather), Arbutus (Madrona) Vaccinium (Blue/Cran/Lingon berries), Rhododendron (and her little sister, Azalea), Oxydendrum (Sourwood) Kalmia (Mountain Laurel), Gaultheria, Zenobia, Pernettya and Pieris.

The Basics: plants that prefer a chalky soil, are species like all roses and many cottage garden bloomers, which came from parts of the world with lots of limestone. Squash and radishes are happier in this corner of the ring. Hydrangea flowers will blush pink in an alkaline soil mix.

VS.

Acid lovers: ericaceous types, especially those native to conifer forests. MOSS — the lowly, root-less variety — can be found in abundance where pH levels are low and acidic. Pour on some buttermilk to encourage moss to conquer that silly lawn. Your Hydrangeas will bloom bluer, too.

Now for some Garden **Physics**. Scientists like to talk about the **behavior** of atoms and molecular substances as if they had thoughts and feelings. Crystals grow, sort of like living creatures and ions have positive or negative charges, causing them to attract or repel one another and create new molecular chains. Every water molecule is composed of two **Hydrogen** atoms and one **Oxygen** atom, represented by the chemical symbol H_2O. Millions of H_2O molecules would fit inside Derek and his sibling, by the way. Water behavior really refers to how those molecules move, and we gardeners are primarily concerned with how they move through soil, making themselves available to our plant roots. Most of our garden's water is being delivered from above, but an underground spring can provide water from below.

Mom!!
Derek pinched me!!

Gravitational Water

deep soaking encourages roots to grow down into a cooler zone

Capillary Action

some seed starts enjoy sitting atop a soggy mat

Gravity is that reassuring force we test every time we drop our keys on the floor. We know that they will go down and not up or sideways. Water will also head downward, mostly, but only if there is enough of it entering the soil in a short period of time. The physical law dictating water's natural movement (in the absence of pressure from a pump or hose nozzle) says that water follows the path of least resistance. Therefore, if it is easier for water to sit on the surface or travel to the side, that is what it will do. To force it down to your plant's thirsty roots, you will need to apply a sufficient amount of water, over a short period, making it heavier.

So: it is better to deeply water your trees with a hose once or twice per week than to have an automatic drip line come on for fifteen or twenty minutes every day. Let gravity do its job for your plants!

Capillary action is the suction that happens when you place a dry sponge at the edge of a puddle on the counter. You can walk away and the sponge will fatten up as it absorbs your spilled lemonade. Dry soil can also act like a sponge and suck water up through the bottom of a pot — don't use lemonade unless you are testing water versus other liquids on the health of potted plants, for your middle school science fair.

Some greenhouse facilities use bottom watering setups to make sure seedling trays never completely dry out. They employ a special fabric called a capillary mat, which holds a lot of water. Pots sitting atop this mat will absorb water through holes in their bottoms, but they will do it slowly, so as not to become too boggy and rot the seedling roots. Capillary mats are handy as houseplant house sitters, if you know you will be unavailable to water your indoor garden for a couple of weeks of vacation.

Drainage is the buzzword, when
it comes to soil-plus-water. Over-watered garden soil will eventually dry out, but some plants can suffer root rot. Drainage in a **container** planting is critical to plant health! Pebbles in the bottom of a pot only make the pot heavier. Don't do it.

The water you pour into the top of a pot will be pulled through the soil by gravity and the roots will take up what they can use. The rest, ideally, escapes down the drain holes. Blocked — or absent!! — holes allow capillary action to pull that excess water back up again, keeping the soil too wet. No soupy saucers, either. Put pebbles in your saucers.

LUCKY YOU!

Lucky four-leaf clover

Lucky penny

once bought you a piece of candy

Lucky rabbit foot

maybe not so lucky for the rabbit

Lucky duck

an old expression

Lucky cookie fortune

Luck. Some people say there's no such thing. Other people knock on wood, cross their fingers, whisper special rhyming phrases, or carry talismans — lucky charms — in their pockets. There is one enormous bit of good fortune that none of us has to leave to chance, rub our lucky crystal or purchase a lottery ticket to obtain. It is the luckiest gift — a priceless jackpot — and billions of plants give it to us every day, for free! That irreplaceable gift is cleaned, **OXYGENATED AIR**.

CO_2 goes in...

O_2 comes out.

Every living, "breathing" plant is an **autotroph**. That means that it is capable of sustaining itself by capturing the sun's heat and energy and converting daylight into food. We animal types rely upon that talent, exclusive to plants. They absorb the carbon dioxide exhaled by every bird, cat, hippo, iguana, orangutan, penguin, koala, giraffe, donkey ... you get the idea — use it to photosynthesize light into lunch and release oxygen back into the atmosphere.

Aerobic respiration is what we are engaged in, 24/7, as we inhale all of that oxygen-rich air and exhale the carbon we can't use. Aerobic exercise, like running, jumping, swimming, and cycling, makes us take in more air. Our lungs and hearts get a workout, and our blood carries more O_2 to every part of our bodies. Even while we sleep our hearts pump the oxygen along, so we don't have to chase rabbits, kicking and barking like our sleeping dogs feel the need to do. That's silly, but fun to watch.

Exercise is more fun when you don't have to.

Anaerobic processes occur in the absence of oxygen. Fermentation — pickling — takes place inside a sealed container, in which an assortment of enzymes digest starches, change the texture and flavor of the plant matter inside. Cider, sauerkraut and pickles come out fizzy. Yeast — a strange, tiny plant form — creates a fermented gas inside dough, making bread rise into a plump loaf.

Plants, of course, are not giving us oxygen out of sheer generosity. It worked out exceptionally well for us that plants can make use of carbon in ways we can't, and as a by product of digesting sunlight, not only supply us with breathable air, but also with a cornucopia of delicious foods and renewable building materials. All they ask from us in return is room to grow. It's important to consider that plants could continue to exist without you and me, but we'd be in serious trouble without them! And they have made enormous progress from the single-celled slime they were, oh about 600 million years ago...

550 million years ago, or so the Earth's surface was still largely underwater. The most complex plants at this point in pre-history were the slimy seaweeds ~ still slimy today - and the sea lilies, which would not make a lovely bouquet. For the next 100 million years plants stayed about this exciting.

Some 445 million years ago rocky land was pushing up through the water. The first life forms to sun themselves out in the open air were the lichens. Algae and fungi joined together to build the strange little colonies we call lichen. They have grown taller over the eras and ages, but have retained their unusual composition.

About 375 million years ago the seas continued to evaporate, exposing more dry land. Mosses and liverworts - but no liverwursts - joined lichens to sun themselves above the waves. No one was putting down roots yet, but they clung to the rocks with sticky "feet", and were not washed away.

Let's say 350 million years ago things really started to get interesting in the plant department. Horsetails ~ most immortal among modern prehistoric weeds ~ and club mosses developed actual roots. Accumulated decaying lichens and crumbling rock provided a thin layer of soil. The first fern fronds unfurled.

Between 300 and 200 million years ago great swamp forests flourished on the land. Trees we would recognize as conifers were abundant. As these cone-bearing trees grew to impressive heights, the first seed-producing plants were beginning to thrive and spread.

Between 200 and 130 million years ago, give or take a few million, dinosaurs munched on trees as though they were stalks of broccoli. The trees outlived the dinos, though, because seeds could survive the extreme freeze of the Ice Age. Those animals that had fur and could burrow underground, fit inside caves or stay underwater made it through that severe climate phase.

The first life forms that could be called animals also lived in the water. Fossils of ancient insects closely resemble some of the creatures that still live under rocks or crawl out of a basement corner today: pillbugs, millipedes, centipedes, silverfish.

the DIRT on SOIL

Pedologists are scientists who study soil. Most of us don't spend a tremendous amount of time thinking about the soil under our feet, unless the rain has turned it into mud that's now stuck on our shoes. If you are a farmer whose soil has lost fertility, you will notice a drop in crop production. If recent construction or remodeling involving heavy vehicles has compacted the topsoil under your new lawn, you will notice an unpleasant squish...squish as you walk across the grass after a heavy rain. If your plants don't seem to be healthy or are growing extremely slowly or if the wind and rain are threatening to wash your hillside away, it is time to consider your soil!

Soil may be as common as muck, but we shouldn't take it for granted. It didn't get here overnight. The outer crust of our planet was once mostly rock, punctuated here and there by lava spouts. When that hot magma from below the surface cooled, it only formed more rock. Over the course of **thousands** of years, rain, running water, wind and melting ice have worn away bits of the mountains of rock, depositing a few inches of the pulverized particles we call soil. Soils vary in mineral composition based on the type of rock from which they originated. They also have special names depending upon how they arrived at their destination. **Residual soil** is what's left of solid rock after the weather has pounded it into crumbs. **Alluvium** is the soil that's been carried along by rivers and streams. **Till** got here as glaciers crept along the continents. **Tilth** is a funny word used to describe the composition, fertility and workability of soil in the context of its ability to support plant growth. Poor soil, poor crops ... poor us!

You can be too rich or too thin. Soil is continually being moved from place to place by people with trucks and mechanical shovels. Sometimes it is excavated — dug up and hauled away — to make space for a building's foundation or basement. That topsoil, which is often pale, dusty and devoid of plant matter, can be mixed with various manures of plant (**humus**) and animal (**poo**) origin and marketed as a bulk or packaged farm or garden product. Soil can become contaminated by airborne toxins and chemical spills, and scientists are studying microbes that may be able to remove all of those poisons. Soil does not belong in the garbage can! Some regional soils naturally contain high concentrations of minerals unsuitable to safely growing crops. Every farmer is a soil scientist!

topsoil
subsoil
rock

Texture is the word we use to refer to the actual mineral composition of a given soil. Soil particles come in an assortment of sizes, from pea gravel, to sharp grains of sand and silt, to the powdery dust that makes up clay. **Loam** is a mixture of all of these particles, and is an ideal basis for plant growth. The addition of **Carbon** (composted manures) make soil dark and rich. Sandy soil drains rapidly and clay stays wet and sticky ~ or dries and cracks in a drought. Never add sand to break up your clay because you will create concrete! **S**tructure is how the combined particles are arranged. There should be some air space between them to allow water flow and let plant roots stretch their toes.

* dirt is what's in your vacuum cleaner

SAGE ADVICE

Science, as we think of it today, is nearly inseparable from technology. Laboratory science takes place in sleek facilities with shiny instruments. Machines with illuminated screens and panels of infinite buttons busily measure, process and report the data that tell us how the world inside and around us works, whether or not we entirely comprehend why. Physical, **applied** science — the phenomena and materials that can be tested and examined repeatedly and somehow put to use in our daily lives ~ has been around for centuries. Before anyone had a career or reputation as a scientist, people who spent their days observing, dissecting and theorizing about the workings of nature and the visible universe were called **philosophers**. Philosophy is still a discipline today, and the word, which translates to "the love of wisdom", could be applied to scientists theorizing about anything we can't actually touch or test — like black holes in deep space — but these days we tend to tie philosophy more closely to the study of human beliefs, than to the movement of the spheres.

Sages were the old wise ones to whom people once turned for advice about how best to live their lives and to gain knowledge about the world's mysteries. Plants, which were every- where, could be seen with the naked eye and had the power to kill or sustain life, alter one's sense of reality, ease suffering and heal ailments, were the province of sages and medicine men. Plants contain oils, terpines, resins and pigments that have been used in ceremonial settings for thousands of years. The aroma from burning dried leaves or their extracts sets a meditative mood and transforms a space. The Native American tradition of burning a dried sagebrush bundle to **smudge**, or cleanse a gathering place has been adopted among non-native practitioners. Sage can produce a lot of smoke — as my smoke alarm has reminded me. Dried sweetgrass also works wonders at transforming a stale environment.

Salvia officinalis is the sage we grind up and use as a cooking herb.

Artemisia tridentata is sagebrush for a smudge stick

Some thoughts for
FOOD

Food: apart from being a word that looks sillier the more you stare at it, food is not a silly subject. We can prepare, present and package our food in fun fashion, but at the most fundamental level, we are what we eat, and if we do not eat, we are **not**. For us, food is an organic (once living) substance providing energy and body-building materials. The plants we eat — and the ones we grow ornamentally — don't eat food, but they do require an assortment of nutrients out of which they build their leaves, stems, flowers and fruit. Plants appear to live on fresh air and sunshine, and they do convert the sun's rays into **carbohydrates**, **fats** and **proteins** through the clever process of **photosynthesis**, which means, 'making something out of light!'

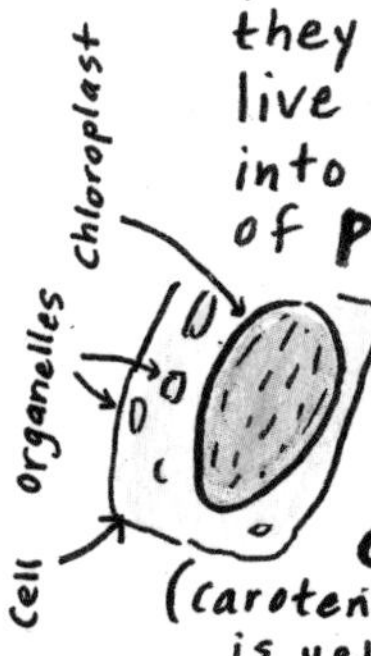

(labels: Cell organelles, Chloroplast)

Every plant comes equipped with **chlorophyll**, the green substance contained within **chloroplasts**, along with **carotene** and **xanthophyll**.
(carotene is orange and xanthophyll is yellow. chlorophyll is darker.)

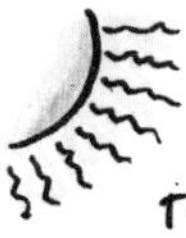

Sunlight energizes these cells' organs, helping them pull in CO_2 (carbon dioxide) and H_2O (water). The chloroplasts then separate and release the O (oxygen) for us to breathe, and combine the remaining H (hydrogen) and C (carbon) into the sugars they "eat"!

Plant Food: if plants create their own dinners by synthesizing sugars and so on inside their own cells, what is inside a package of **fertilizer**?

Add to your daily diet of CO_2, H_2O and sunlight. Serving size: one half teaspoon per square foot of newly planted soil, if you are a fresh sprout. More if you can already see over the top of the pot.

Special **NPK** *Ol'loggs*
an important part of this and every other day's nutritious breakfast, lunch and dinner!
1 TSP
Tastes like dirt!
20-20-20

N is for **Nitrogen**. It comes from ammonia, which is why packaged fertilizer smells a lot like a busy litter pan. By the time a plant has taken N up through its roots and filters it through its tissues, the ammonia smell is gone, so you won't taste it in your green peas, spinach or lettuce, none of which can become green without the help of Nitrogen.

P is for **Phosphorous**. P builds strong bones in people, and sturdy leaves and stems in plants. A box of Bone Meal is the most concentrated source of P. Helps build strong plant bodies so plants can help build strong people bodies.

K is for **Potassium**. (I know, so why is it K and not "P"? It's that Greco-Roman/Latin scientific naming thing at work again.) K fattens up roots, but also supports flower, seed and fruit development. P + K = blooms.

N-P-K are the "big three" elements of the fertilizer world, and they are represented in that order, by percentage of content, on any box or bag you buy. They are the **macronutrients**, but plants also need **micronutrients**: Fe (iron), Mg (magnesium), Cu (copper), Zn (zinc), B (boron), Mo (molybdenum), Mn (manganese), plus some **trace elements**: Cl (chlorine), Na (sodium), Si (silicon), Al (aluminum), and Co (cobalt). Just pour and add milk — I mean H_2O!

what comes around GROWS AROUND

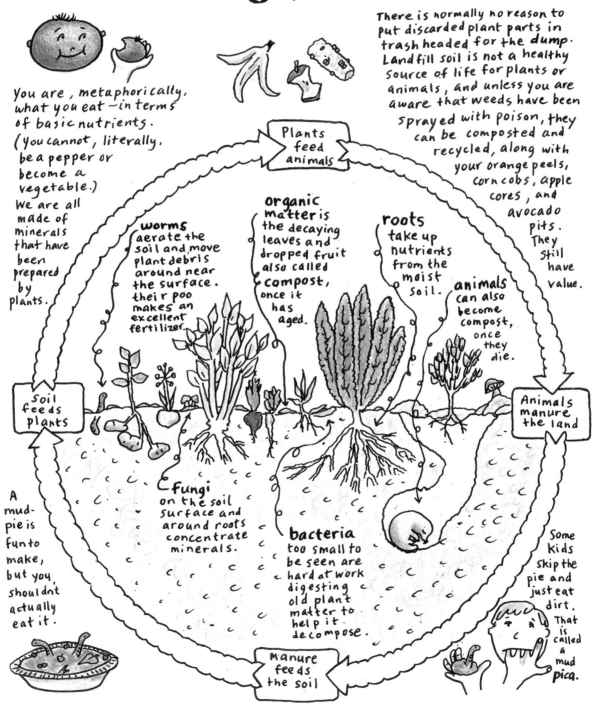

You are, metaphorically, what you eat — in terms of basic nutrients. (You cannot, literally, be a pepper or become a vegetable.) We are all made of minerals that have been prepared by plants.

There is normally no reason to put discarded plant parts in trash headed for the dump. Landfill soil is not a healthy source of life for plants or animals, and unless you are aware that weeds have been sprayed with poison, they can be composted and recycled, along with your orange peels, corn cobs, apple cores, and avocado pits. They still have value.

Plants feed animals

worms aerate the soil and move plant debris around near the surface. their poo makes an excellent fertilizer.

organic matter is the decaying leaves and dropped fruit also called compost, once it has aged.

roots take up nutrients from the moist soil.

animals can also become compost, once they die.

Soil feeds plants

Animals manure the land

Fungi on the soil surface and around roots concentrate minerals.

bacteria too small to be seen are hard at work digesting old plant matter to help it decompose.

A mud-pie is fun to make, but you shouldn't actually eat it.

Some kids skip the pie and just eat dirt. That is called a mud pica.

Manure feeds the soil

Budding Beauty

"*Hope springs eternal.*" That's a very old expression. Here is another: "*where there's life, there's hope.*" Hope is what spring is all about, and when we step out into the garden after winter has finally gone, we can take a close look at what our trees and shrubs are up to. The spring season officially begins in late March, where many gardens may still be covered in snow. April is more famous for showers, but by May, all danger of frost should be over, and there should be an abundance of leaves and flowers in view. Some trees put out flowers first, on "bare wood", followed by leaves in a few weeks. What you may not have noticed before the appearance of all that color were the quiet, unassuming **buds**. If there were no buds, there would be no leaves or flowers. Just what is a bud? How did it get there, and what happens when you pick them off? What do **bugs** have to do with buds?

THIS IS A LEAF OF THE SCOTCH ELM (Ulmus glabra)
Striate-scaled, Imbricate Bud (Dentate leaf)

LEAF BUD

THIS IS A BRAND-NEW ELM LEAF, ABOUT TO UNFOLD

THESE ARE BUD SCALES, DROPPING AWAY TO REVEAL THE NEW LEAF

THIS MARK IS A BUD-SCALE SCAR LEFT BY THE BASE OF LAST YEARS LEAF AFTER IT FELL IN THE GREAT FALL (AUTUMN)

Sometimes it seems as if a tree is bare wood one day and covered in leaves the next. Once bud scales are shed, new leaves unfold very quickly. They open out, soft and pale green, or almost yellow, but they will toughen up and darken now that they are exposed to sunlight. Not every tree has green leaves, but even purple and red ones start out paler.

Evergreen leaves also begin life as buds, but their openings and departures are more staggered, so new growth makes a less dramatic appearance.

Next year's leaf buds form in autumn, just above this year's hard working and exhausted leaves, which are ready to take their leave. Inside those tightly wrapped buds, tender leaf tissue will be protected by scales from winter's chill. If you pick those brownish buds off ~ perhaps believing they are insects ~ new leaves will still have a chance to form in spring, but they will be delayed, and the tree will be hungry while it catches up (so don't be like that silly customer I once had).

Leaf buds vary in shape from one species to another and can provide a helpful identification key while the tree is dormant, as in March and November, when the WA State Nursery Professionals exam is offered. (Bark helps, too.)

WILLOW (Salix)
One-scaled Bud
(Simple leaf)

WHITE ASH (Fraxinus)
Rounded Bud
(Compound leaf)

SCRUB OAK (Quercus)
Accessory Bud
(Lobed leaf)

"*Position in life is everything.*" That's another old adage, but there are varying outcomes for buds, depending upon their location on the tree. Plants are set up with an internal directive called **apical dominance.** An **apex** (plural: **apices**), is the highest point on the plant. This will come up again when we talk about pruning, but it has a lot to do with how and where the tree directs its growth. Every branch has an apex, too, where you will find the **terminal** bud. All other buds along the branch are known as **lateral** buds. The goal of the tree is to **grow.** Not only does each bud contain a leaf preparing to feed the existing tree, it also sits atop the potential to sprout a new branch. If every bud put out a branch, the tree would quickly become an overcrowded tangle.

The terminal bud determines how long a branch will grow. If the terminal bud becomes damaged or gets removed, energy goes to the lateral buds instead, and the tree will grow wider. A missing bud here or there is not a big deal, but if every terminal bud is gone ~ as in shearing ~ things will really start to go pear-shaped, or perhaps it would be more appropriate to say, shrub-shaped. Pinching out a young lateral branch is the kindest way to prevent that branch from growing into the right-of-way or into your own way. Pinch off too many terminal buds, and you will have a blob.

Leaf buds appear at regular intervals. If you ever spot a random cluster of shiny brown bumps resembling bud scales, your plant has been infested by Terrapin scale, a destructive insect and plant part impostor! An application of horticultural oil will smother this opportunistic garden pest.

Every leaf has a means of attaching to the plant. A stem or stalk provides that connection and also the plumbing through which food travels down into the branch and water and minerals up into the leaf. The scientific name for that connecting stalk is the **petiole.** Most of a leaf's bulk is the **blade,** a term most people attach to a single grass leaf, but even a Catalpa leaf as big as your face is a blade. A **simple** leaf has only one blade per petiole, while a **compound** leaf has multiple blades, called **leaflets,** attached along a central stem called a **rachis.**

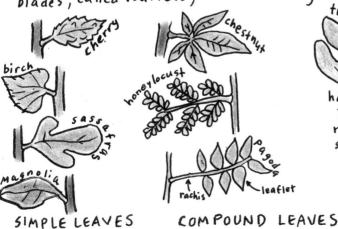

SIMPLE LEAVES — cherry, birch, sassafras, magnolia

COMPOUND LEAVES — chestnut, honeylocust, pagoda, rachis, leaflet

tulip tree has a simple leaf with rather oddly shaped lobes

SORT OF SIMPLE LEAVES...

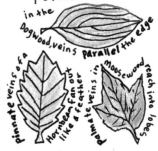

There are also characteristic variations in the way veins branch out from a leaf's petiole.

in the Dogwood, veins parallel the edge

pinnate veins of a Hornbeam fan out like a feather

palmate veins in a Moosewood reach into lobes

the Art of Flower Arrangement

"Don't panicle," said the
wise old peduncle.

Was it a **panicle**, or a **corymb**?
If anyone knew, it would be him!
It could be an **umbel**, or maybe a **cyme**?
No, neither of those —
It's a **spike**, this time.

*F*loral arranging is a decorative manner of displaying cut flower stems. Florists use vases of assorted shapes, sometimes with a block of dense floral foam at the bottom to hold the stems upright. Japanese flower arrangement, called **Ikebana** employs small, spiked "frogs", which grab small stems. It is a temporary, living sculpture.

*N*ature, of course, set about arranging flowers long before people were around to pick them, but it is people who observe and give names to the natural order of things, including floral structure.

*S*pike flower heads look like a little flagpole, with individual blossoms attached in a series along the entire length.

the flowers of **Veronica spicata** grow this way, with each flower stuck directly to the main stalk (no pedicel).

Cymes are comprised of individual florets that radiate from a perch atop the central stalk, forming a flat array around it.

← floret

*R*acemes carry their blooms serially, like spikes, but each one attaches by a **pedicel**, and the visual effect is less stiff.

Wisteria racemes hang gracefully upside-down overhead, gently perfuming the air while twining tendrils work their mischief around the gutters, tree branches and slow walkers.

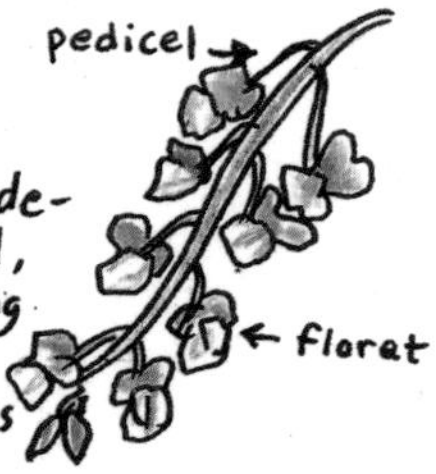

pedicel →

← floret

Study an "annual" **Pelargonium**, or hothouse Geranium and you will find that its "flower" is actually a cyme of multiple, dainty florets. Okay- semi dainty.

Umbels are easy to recognize because they resemble inside-out umbrellas. Every plant in the carrot family, **Umbelliferae**, which includes parsley, celery, Queen Anne's Lace, dill, fennel and sweet Cicely — among others — bears its blooms in umbels.

Butterflies like to sip nectar from umbels, as do wasps and bumble bumbles.

Corymbs are similar to umbels and cymes, with florets curving toward a central stalk via pedicels. A corymb's pedicels don't all attach near the tip of the stalk, but rather for some distance along it in a random, ladder-like arrangement.

Plums and cherries, both in the genus **Prunus**, display their flowers and then fruit in corymbs.

Panicles are lush, thick clusters of multiple racemes sharing the same stalk, or multiple spikes, or corymbs, or cymes or umbels sharing one stalk. The result is a heavy, generously populated and impressive floral presence. Add some fragrance to a panicle, and it may get overwhelming. Perfumed or not, panicles stand out by a mile.

Hydrangea paniculata's name gives away its arrangement.

Solitary flowers sit all alone at the tip of a stalk, but are seldom lonely, as they have all-day visiting hours and plenty of admirers, too, among insects, birds and us.

Composite flowers — recall the illustrious Daisy/**Aster** family — also attach to the stem in solitary fashion. Each flower is a two part **head**, unlike the blooms of a **Rose** or **Magnolia** — pictured to the left — each one a truly solitary, individual beauty.

So, what, exactly is a **peduncle**? That is the scientific name for the central stalk by which a **pedicel** is joined to the branch or stem of a tree or bedding plant. They are all stems of a sort, at the end of the day, and it certainly sounds nicer to the ear to refer to a dozen 'long-stemmed' roses than it would to say a bouquet of fragrant 'long-peduncled' lilacs. Latin is for plant lovers, but not the loveliest language!

POLLEN COUNTS.

Pollen, in our noses and sinus passages can make us miserable. On those days when tapping a branch of the cedar tree sends out thick clouds of yellow dust, it is best to stay indoors with the windows shut and the air cleaner humming. For the worst hay fever sufferers, pollen can seem like a cruel enemy. In truth, pollen is one of our dearest friends. It has sustained plant reproduction for millions of years, continues to get the job done and isn't going away anytime soon. Let's take a closer — and then a much closer — look at the secrets of pollen.

Stamens are a flower's pollen factory. Pollen grains develop inside the anther at the tip of each filament that grows out of the center of a flower. Some flowers have stamens alone, and are called **male** flowers. A plant with only **stamenate** flowers belongs to a species that is called **dioecious**, meaning that the female flowers are found on their own plant, in a separate household. Co-habitating flowers belong to **monecious** species. Take a peek inside a flower — they aren't shy.

Pistils are topped by a sticky pad called a stigma. Pollen is delivered to each stigma, typically by a bee or wasp who has previously visited several other flowers in search of a meal of nectar. You have likely seen a bee whose legs are coated in yellow powder. Wind also distributes pollen — think of those overwhelming cedar cones — and grasses, in particular are wind-pollinated. Corn is a grass, which is why you don't see bees hanging around it. **Pistillate** flowers are female, and once sufficiently pollinated will develop fruit — either dry seeds or delicious, fleshy, juicy plums and such — in their hidden ovaries. Some plants, such as strawberries, have multiple pistils per flower but most flowers have one each. A monecious flower has a group of stamens surrounding a central pistil.

Cistus blossom with a pistil flanked by anthers

Most flowers are attractive to us as well as to the bees, and we add them to our gardens for color and fragrance. Flowers put on a show to draw insects near, because they rely upon pollen transfer to form seeds for future generations. Every plant has some kind of reproductive structure. Flowers so small or plain that we barely notice them are referred to as insignificant, but they matter to the plant, and to the insects that stop by for a meal. Many early spring bloomers, often with icky-smelling, small white flowers, are pollinated by flies, because it's still too chilly for new bees to hatch out of their winter hives.

pollen generator

fruit factory

Actinidia (Kiwi) flower on male vine

and its friend on a female vine

Fruit does not happen without pollination. You can have an apple tree covered in flowers, but if the bees fail to visit no fruit will form in the flowers' ovaries. In addition to pollination — the physical transfer of pollen from anther to stigma — some plant species or cultivars (hybrids) require something called **pollenization**. That means they require pollen from a closely related plant, but not one of the identical hybrid. You may notice that when you shop for apples in the grocery store there are many varieties of apple, each with a specific name. All of those names

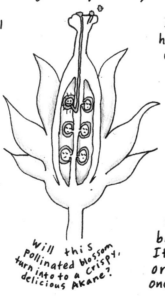

'Red Delicious' x 'Ralls Janet' **'Fuji'**

'Golden Delicious' x 'Lady Williams' **'Pink Lady'**

chance hybrid x of wild and domesticated apples **'Granny Smith'**

'Enterprise' x 'Honeycrisp' **'Cosmic Crisp'**

'Royal Gala' x 'Braeburn' **'Jazz'**

indicate that the trees were developed by horticulturalists through genetic crosses to produce a unique apple with improved flavor, juiciness and crisp bite. Every one of these apples tastes better than the humble wild fruits that people plucked several hundred years ago. It also means that a Fuji apple tree will not successfully pollinate, or pollenize another Fuji. Orchardists, who specialize in growing fruit crops, need to plant an assortment of apple varieties to serve as pollenizers for one another. For backyard growers who don't have the space for multiple trees, grafted trees can be planted. You can plant a single tree — mine grows Spartan, Akane and Chehalis apples.

Pollination is successful when a pollen grain sticks to the stigma and tunnels via a newly-formed pollen tube down into the flower's ovary. Inside the ovary the ova (eggs - one is an ovum) are sleeping. Once pollen reaches an ovum and fertilizes it, a fruit will begin to develop. If insufficient or incompatible pollen has been deposited, a puny fruit or no fruit at all will form, and the flower will drop from the plant.

Will this pollinated blossom turn into to a crispy, delicious Akane?

During seasons when my trees have been in full bloom but I'm worried about the absence of bees, I have taken a small, soft-tipped paintbrush and pollinated my apples, pears and cherries. That means taking some Chehalis pollen and brushing it on a Spartan blossom, and so forth. The cherry is a self-pollenizing variety, meaning that it is satisfied with its own pollen, but it is not self-pollinating. It still needs a wasp or a bee or me to move the pollen from one flower to another.

Micrographs are photographs taken through a microscope. Captured this way, pollen grains resemble weird, alien spacecraft. When you view them in such close-ups, it's easy to understand why they irritate our eyes and noses so.

Ulmus (Elm)

Justicia (Shrimp Plant)

Polygala (Milkwort)

Crossandra (Firecracker Flower)

COME TOWARD THE LIGHT

WHAT ON EARTH

WE ARE YOUR FRIENDS, HORMO

OH! I MUST STOP EATING BEAN SPROUTS AT BED-TIME!

RISE AND SHINE, YOUNG MAN. THE SUN IS UP.

Let's talk a bit about the SUN and the effect it has upon life, both plant and human. Light, or its absence triggers nearly every process that happens inside a plant's tissues. What our eyes can't see is that there, inside the cells, are chemicals responding to light. These chemicals are called **hormones**, and they direct the plant's movement. That doesn't mean that if someone opens the fridge door the Rubber Tree will shuffle across the kitchen for a midnight snack (although that crazy ant might give it a try).

Phototropism. Photo means light. A photograph is an image created when light bounces off an object and onto a light-sensitive surface. **Tropos**, in turn, is Greek for **turn**. Plants will turn toward the brightest available source of light, particularly if it is daylight, which they crave.

This all-too familiar and pathetic sight is the *Dracaena marginata*, sitting in a pot for years across the room from a window. No one thought to rotate the pot once in a while or to set it closer to the window. They are frequent inmates of restaurants, doctors' offices and bank lobbies, where they are meant to be cheerful but somehow fail at that aim.

The hormone reacting to the light is called **auxin**, Greek for **increase**. When light hits the stem tips, cells will extend in length. A branch will actually s t r e t c h toward the light. Plants grown in low light environments develop long **internodes** — the spaces between each successive leaf or branch origin, as they reach to find sufficient **photo** in order to **photo**synthe**size**. We have already talked about the process of photosynthesis, the magic that plants do with light and chlorophyll.

Gibberellin is the hormone determining internodal distances. If you take two identical plant starts and play evil scientist — perhaps for the science fair, or perhaps because you have a basement bedroom ~ and give one more light than the other, this is what you will see:

You will not grow taller (or shorter) in the basement, but you probably should get outside more.

Specimen grown in your basement laboratory has long internodes

Specimen grown upstairs has shorter internodes and larger, darker green leaves, as well.

If you are lucky you may get a chance to witness phototropism in action, without time-lapse photography. On one of those days when the wind was rapidly carrying some thick clouds across the sky, the light levels changed so dramatically from one minute to the next that I caught one of my houseplants perking up and raising its sleepy branches as the light level temporarily brightened. It was one of those rare, fascinating moments like being out in a snow flurry while wearing a navy blue wool coat and being able to clearly see individual snowflakes.

Photoperiodism controls how plants respond to changing day length. Tropical plants grow near the **equator**, where the sun always reaches high overhead and day and night duration is consistent year-round. Farther from the equator, in the **temperate** zones, days are longer during the summer months and shorter in winter, as Earth's elliptical orbit takes us a longer distance from the sun. The contrast is especially noticeable in places like Barrow, Alaska ~ very far from the equator! ~ where my friend, Galen spent entire childhood winters in endless nighttime mode. Seasonal transitions, for most of us, happen gradually, and plants rely on the slow adjustment to increasing daylight hours to plan such activities as blooming, releasing pollen, and setting seed, just as birds know when to lay eggs. **Florigen** is the hormone that regulates this seasonal activity in plant brains. Artificial light and controlled day length in greenhouses is the secret to year-round cut-flower production and the appearance of Poinsettias at christmastime.

North

Tomorrow may rain,
so I'll follow the sun.

West   East

South

Nastic movements are often depicted in time-lapse nature films that show a seedling pushing up through the soil and swinging from side to side as if it were dancing. Many vines attach themselves to vertical structures by circling and twining themselves around repeatedly. Although this motion would seem to have something to do with the daily movement of the sun, that appears to be a myth (like the theory that water in the Northern Hemisphere spirals in the opposite to water in the Southern Hemisphere when you flush the toilet). Twining motion, or tracing invisible circles in the air is just a weird, groovy thing that plants do.

What about people and light? Sunlight on our skin helps our bodies produce what we call VitaminD. Sunshine is psychologically uplifting, and after extended weeks of overcast, cloudy skies some people say they feel "blue", but by replacing yellowish, 'warm white' lightbulbs with bluer, full-spectrum 'cool white' lightbulbs, you can feel more alert in your imitation daylight and avert S.A.D. ~ Seasonal Affective Disorder. We are, it appears, drawn to light in other ways, like a moth's irresistible urge to circle a flame. We spend countless hours in the thrall of projected light and in the glow of L.E.D.s ~ the Light Emitting Diodes beaming from ever-present screens!

streaming movies on monitors

doing work, homework, surfing, reading - doom-scrolling

sucked in by flashing marquee

BIG SALE

talking to the BFF right next to you by texting

IS THERE LIFE ON MARS?

Venus Flytraps do not come from Venus, and only moon rocks live on the Moon. Whether there is or ever was anything we might legitimately call *life* on the planet we call **Mars** (its inhabitants would have an entirely different name for it, assuming they have language) and whether Mars could sustain human life remains to be seen. Certain more adventurous (and absurdly wealthy) types than myself have set their sights on not merely visiting, but colonizing that planet, and the best of luck to the three of them. We stick-in-the-mud types will stick to our familiar mud here on Earth, with all its faults, gravity, moody climate, raging tides, temperamental volcanoes and all of that **atmosphere**. Why? It is precisely the atmosphere, with its layers of breathable air that allowed life as we know it to exist on this planet. I don't know about you, but I greatly appreciate being able to inhale approximately every seven seconds, taking for granted the fact that I am surrounded by abundant, free-range **OXYGEN**, the wonderstuff we evolved over the course of five hundred or so million years to breathe.

N.A.S.A. has sent plants into space with its astronauts, to provide extra oxygen and also to take advantage of plants' air-cleaning abilities. Spacecraft air is finite and it recirculates for the entire voyage.

Oxygen is available in large enough quantity to keep you alive and breathing **only within two miles** above Earth's surface. Don't leave **Home** without your space-suit and a generous tank of air.

Every living thing on Earth contains **Carbon. Organic chemistry** concerns itself with the study of all substances built of carbon compounds. Charcoal is created by burning wood, and softer wood makes softer charcoal. Coal results from wood or charcoal that has been compressed underground, into soft rock, beginning as long as 400 million years ago. Layer upon layer of decaying plant and simple animal matter packed together and squeezed into coal. The greater the weight of water, soil and new life above on the surface, the firmer the resulting coal became. The planet's oldest coal was largely formed from **ferns** and **mosses**. Even the youngest coal formed over 250 million years ago, and archaeologists, who excavate and study the remains of long-gone civilizations have shown that people burned coal at least 4,000 years ago. We continue to mine it from deposits near the surface or down dangerous shafts reaching into deposits more than 250 feet down. Much of the world still depends upon the energy derived by burning coal ~ and other carbon-origin **fossil fuels** ~ even as we are catching up to the realization that we, as a global population, will have to figure out a less damaging alternative. We love our carbon, we are carbon, but we also love to breathe clean air, and if we do not love our planet, where else can we go? If you said, "Mars", you get a lump of coal.

Carbon-rich ferns and cycads photosynthesized and packed their cells with energy. The earliest animals ate leaves from these plants

Plants, and the animals that ate them, died and decayed in swamps and bogs

Coal deposits are mined commercially throughout the Northern Hemisphere.

It is transported thousands of miles and used to make many products

If you are reading this as a kid, I hope that by the time you are old enough to be reading to your own child, energy use on Earth will have struck a sufficient balance between carbon-based fossil fuels and renewable, sustainable resources. At this particular moment, too much of the planet is burning up, literally (wildfires) and figuratively (broken high temperature records). Fire consumes both carbon and oxygen, but carbon-dioxide, compressed inside the canister of a fire extinguisher, can put out the flames. Coal is a commodity that still remains in vast quantities, deep below the surface. There are entire communities, towns and even counties whose people depend upon the coal industry for their livelihoods. They will need alternative employment to feed their families. Fire will never become obsolete. It is not a substance but a reaction that happens when the combination of flammable materials reaches a certain temperature and the ideal concentration of oxygen oxidizes those materials. Add a spark and it's fire.

Ancient history: twentieth century America!! I am 'Mid-Century Modern', so some of these antiquated practices took place during my earliest decades. Not the first one, though. I come from a long, continuous line of tiny women but I never met Bella Berkowitz.

UTAH KING COAL Lasts Longer

A LITTLE RUSTY AROUND THE EDGES.

My great-grandmother, Bella had to shovel coal into the furnace in the cellar each morning, to heat the radiators in the store and the rooms above. Tommy the alley cat dispatched any mice.

Bella's daughter, Pearl, sold the store in the early 1960's and moved into a modern building, also in Brooklyn. I remember going down the hall with her to a closet where she opened a chute and sent the garbage down to be burned in the incinerator.

Pearl's granddaughter, Linda (me) lives in a house that was built in 1928. It originally had a coal furnace in the dug-out cellar. While digging along my fenceline I unearthed some old metal signs, set in place as edging. Merry.

Business end down, dear.

Chapter Six

Garden Care and Safekeeping

The Gloves are On

Cover Story

magazine

FALL Special ISSUE

Your SOIL is SHOWING!

- WHY YOU SHOULD COVER IT UP
- THIS YEAR'S TIPS ON COVER CROP FASHIONS

A Well-made Bed.

much ado about mulching:

it's just the thing to do! Finally — a good use for all those fallen leaves — but don't mulch with:
- Grass clippings with seed heads — not in flowerbeds!
- Weed tops with their taproots attached.
- Weeds that have been chemically sprayed.
- Weeds like conifer needles.
- Acidic leaves like conifer needles.
- Old, smelly socks — but dryer lint is okay.

A mulch a day keeps the weeds at bay!

Don't leave room for weeds.

More ways to Love your FAVA BEANS

Cover crops to know and Sow : green manure to add to

veggie beds, now! You can enjoy the edible beans in spring and then chop and "tuck the plants in" under the soil to enrich it for the new season. You can plant some of the new beans, to start another round. Other great cover crops to start from seed are Lacy Phacelia, oats, wild peas, mustard greens and clover.

Forgot to sow a cover crop? You can keep weeds out with layers of newsprint (black ink, please) or cardboard.

Always make amends!

Don't put your garden to bed angry! Friendly soil makes better plants. Give your soil some mycorrhizae. Some fresh soil microbes and a serving of compost will give your earthworms a snack. Keep everybody cozy with a warm blanket of mulch.

How you can stay in CLOVER

It's a lucky garden that has been planted with nitrogen-rich clover. Red, white, purple or yellow, the bees will love the nectar. (and the bunnies like clover, too)

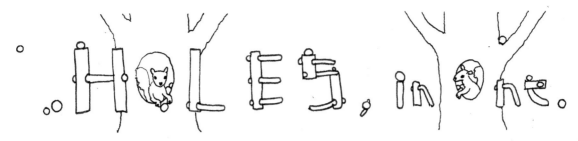

HOLES, in One.

Everything we plant requires a planting hole, from the tiny ones you will make for a seed, to the spooned-out spot for a veggie "plug" and up to the serious crater your large tree will require. If you are just sowing seeds directly into the ground, and the soil has been loosened up first, all you need to make your holes is a small bamboo stick. You don't have to remove any soil. Save the soil you dig out for your big plants, because some of it will be going back into the hole, along with a little bit of compost. Unless, like me, you are trying to create your own forest, your digging tasks shouldn't be too daunting. Most shrubs and trees are sold in pots no larger than ten gallons worth of soil, but if your garden has no shade and you really need your tree to be big right away, you will be welcomed to the world of the Balled and Burlapped! This is where all of the field-grown trees come from, the ones that get planted on school campuses and office parks and road sides and shopping malls. They are everywhere!

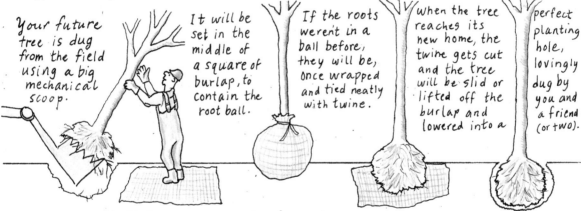

Your future tree is dug from the field using a big mechanical scoop.

It will be set in the middle of a square of burlap, to contain the root ball.

If the roots weren't in a ball before, they will be, once wrapped and tied neatly with twine.

When the tree reaches its new home, the twine gets cut and the tree will be slid or lifted off the burlap and lowered into a

perfect planting hole, lovingly dug by you and a friend (or two).

Burlap is an itchy cloth made from jute fiber. It is popular with coffee and potato growers, and typically smells oddly musty. It has long been used for wrapping tree roots because it "breathes" and absorbs water, and also because it biodegrades. Even though that means it would eventually break down in the soil, your tree will be happier if you don't put the burlap into the planting hole. All you want to put into that hole, besides the effort you put into digging it, is that hefty root ball, enough **soil** to fill the gap around the roots, perhaps a light sprinkling of natural **fertilizer**, and a generous drink of **water**. If you want to **stake** your tree for support, read on!

HIGH STAKES MISTAKES: The purpose of staking a new tree is to keep it from blowing over in the wind while it is rooting in.

Growers stake trees like this, to protect them in transit. Please free this poor tree from its bonds once you get it in the ground.

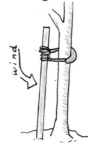

wind

You can install that stake on the windward side of your tree. Wrap soft or stretchy cord several times around the stake, but never run rings of twine around the tree.

Another way is to use two short stakes. Tree trunks need to flex to grow strong. Remove all stakes and ties after two years.

CANOPIES: The lush, leafy, shady tree tops are also called the tree canopy. A tree chosen to provide shade for a picnic ground or patio will have a wide, or broadly-spreading canopy. The grower has removed lower branches to make room for you and your family to picnic below.

In the days before plastic was used for everything, trees were sold in cans! The open, metal cans were difficult to remove, and had to be cut open with tin snips.

Can O' Peas

Plastic pots are flexible, but if you are struggling to coax your tree out of its pot, it may help to gently lay it on its side. One of you can sit and bounce a bit to loosen the root ball

while your teammate carefully tugs on the trunk,

Sliding the tree out of the pot.

It isn't often that difficult to de-pot a plant, unless it's pot-bound, which means it spent too long in the can. If you can't poke a trowel into the surface of the soil, the roots are overgrown. Your tree is not past its sell-by date (unlike those peas in the back of the pantry since 2003) but it will need some extra root care. If they are going in a circle around the outer edge of the ball, cut into them with a pair of pruners. Pull the cut ends outward, so they won't keep going round and round, forever!

You should see about ½ soil to ½ pale roots.

Circling roots will keep on circling, even in the ground.

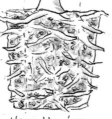

Here they've been cut and fanned out, so they can spread.

Unless you are digging a pond, the largest holes you will have to dig will be for trees. Everything else you plant will take less work! Gone are the days when a tree hole had to be the size of a compact car or a tetherball court. That's not because trees are different than they were twenty years ago, but because tree people have determined that it's better to let the roots do their own work of breaking out beyond the planting hole and reaching their way under your yard. Eventually, that network of roots will be wider than the leafy canopy overhead, and at least half as deep as your grown-up tree is tall. That's important, because with a tiny, circling root system, even a stake won't save your tree from a high wind.

← CROWN

THIS HOLE IS TOO SMALL.

THIS HOLE IS TOO BIG.

THIS HOLE IS JUST RIGHT.

CROWNS: Your crown is on the top of your head, but in the plant world, the crown is the point where the roots meet the trunk, or whichever portion of the plant belongs above ground. It is easiest to see in woody plants — the trees and shrubs — and it's important for the health of the trunk not to bury that crown. It should sit just at the ground's surface or slightly above it. If you sink the crown in the soil or under too much mulch, the trunk's base can get rotten and weak. Trees that break off from their roots are often victims of rotting crowns.

DIGGING TIPS: If you are making lots of holes at once, you may be able to save yourself some effort, if your plants will be close together. Loosen an area with your garden **fork**. Create a small trench, add a bit of compost, arrange your plants in the trench and fill around them with soil. Plants from larger pots go in first, then you can add back a bit of soil to raise the level for your smaller starts. This approach works well for bulb planting, too, and ensures a loose, weed-free patch.

A VERY MIXED BORDER

Let's ♠ Call a Spade a Spade ♠

Shall we? Whether or not you dig gardening, most gardening tasks are going to involve digging, sooner or later. The first big tool a typical beginning gardener will ask for is a "shovel", and they are on the right track, but a shovel is best used to shove a substance such as snow, gravel or coal. When you want to break ground and create a planting hole what you are really looking for is a "spade".

Garden **spades** come in a few different shapes and sizes. A flat-blade spade is good for edging or cutting straight lines. A rounded or pointed blade is best for digging deeper holes. Transplanting spades are narrow-bladed for getting into small spaces. All have long handles and are designed to be used while standing.

Heigh **hoe**, heigh hoe. There are several styles of hoe. This one is a scuffle or "hula" hoe, which when scratched back and forth will loosen weeds and cut off their tops.

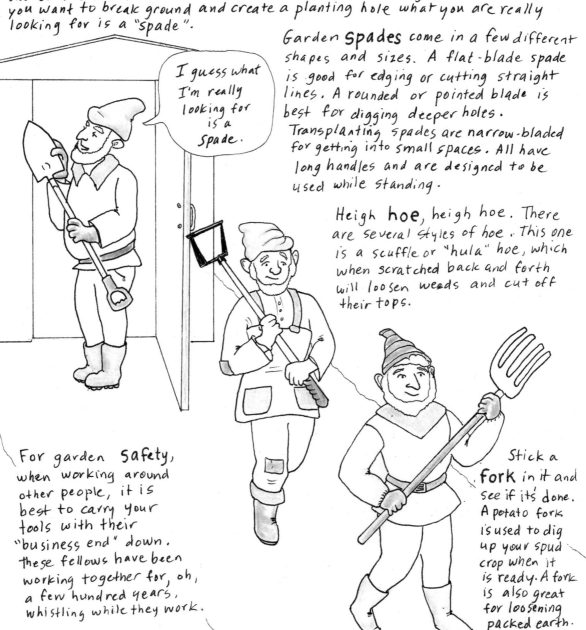

I guess what I'm really looking for is a spade.

For garden **safety**, when working around other people, it is best to carry your tools with their "business end" down. These fellows have been working together for, oh, a few hundred years, whistling while they work.

Stick a **fork** in it and see if it's done. A potato fork is used to dig up your spud crop when it is ready. A fork is also great for loosening packed earth.

A **rake's** progress. A flat-head rake is very strong and can be used to level-out soil, gravel and mulch. The teeth are perfect for gathering up leaves, acorns and other plant debris.

Cultivating a new hobby. A **cultivator** looks a bit like a back scratcher. This one is a three-fingered, or pronged type, and scratching is what it does, but in the soil. It is good for breaking up clumps and also for pulling up weeds. A roto-tiller is another kind of cultivator with rows of spinning teeth.

For the **shear** fun of it. A long-handled, sharp-bladed clipper is great for cutting neatly through hedge tips and grasses. Shears are not designed for use when you are pruning off thick branches. To do that job, you want a pair of loppers, which are long-handled pruners. The long handles let you use your arms, for more strength per cut.

The **pick** of the crop. One way to break new ground when it is rocky or hard is with a pick-axe, or mattock. This job can be rather hard on the elbows and is therefore best done in limited amounts, or with the tireless help of small, fictional people, such as garden gnomes.

P-PATCH

BUCKET BRIGADE

The rains have stopped, and your garden is thirsty. How are you planning to "be a cloud" and bring them the water you know they will need?

Firstly, your SOURCE:

the TAP,
in your kitchen or bathroom.

If you are watering your houseplants, this is your most likely water source.

If you happen to have a garden **rain barrel**, or **cistern**, collected rainwater is the preferred beverage of such treasures as **orchids**, **flytraps** and **pitcher plants**, as well as **bromeliads**, who do not seem to enjoy all of the flouride and chlorine in most tapwater. If you don't have a way to collect or store rain water, you can give them charcoal-filtered water or bottled drinking water.

saddle up your hose

the BIB,
not just for babies, although it sometimes dribbles. If it makes you giggle to call it a **bib**, you can use the word **spigot** or **faucet**. Some bibs have a saddle on top, for hanging a hose.

An outdoor faucet is the way to go, for extensive watering. You can fill up a bucket or attach a hose. It is always a good idea to shut the water off at the bib when you are done, and not leave the hose to take all that pressure. You only need to experience one burst hose in order to learn that valuable lesson.

the WELL,
mostly for wishing or decoration, but still a vital destination for many populations without indoor plumbing setups.

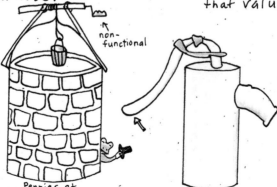

non-functional

Pennies at bottom, but no talking frogs.

the PUMP,
another old-fashioned way to get water out of the ground. Crank the lever up and down until water comes out.

Secondly, your DELIVERY METHOD:

the CAN,

also known as a **bucket, pot or pail**. It's good to have more than one, or at least an indoor and an outdoor can. Keep one for clean water only, as you don't want to fill your bird bath or pet bowl with fertilizer residue!

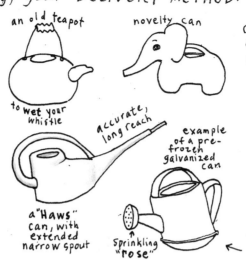

an old teapot
to wet your whistle

novelty can

accurate, long reach

a "Haws" can, with extended narrow spout

example of a pre-frozen galvanized can

Sprinkling "rose"

Watering cans come in many styles and materials. For small potted plants, you want a narrow spout. To water tiny seedlings gently you should attach a **rose**. Empty your outdoor cans for winter and store them someplace warm, or any water left inside can freeze, warping or splitting the metal. My first can rocks and rolls.

the HOSE,

originally a hose "pipe", as in a pipe made of fabric or other flexible material, like a firehose. If you use a hose to water your edibles, you should look for one that has been rated "drinking water safe". If the water that comes out of your hose smells toxic, it most likely is toxic. Yuck.

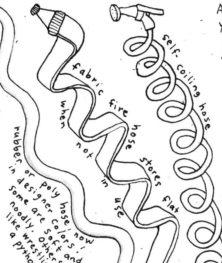

rubber or poly hose / now in designer colors! some are soft and noodly, others feel like wrestling a python.

fabric fire hose when not in use

self-coiling hose stores flat

Attach a **nozzle** to your hose to make the flow adjustable. Some nozzles only control how much water comes out, but others have lots of options, like mist, powerwash, shower, fan or stream. A soft mist feels great on a hot day!

easy on-off thumb control!

A rubber soaker hose has pinholes along its length so water can weep and seep slowly into your flower beds.

the DRIP,

an elaborate system of tubes and connectors Spaced emitters - probes in the soil or sprinkler heads - will deliver water only to desired spots, or into your pots. They can be attached to automatic timers, so your plants won't dry out while you are busy or away.

Be careful not to mow the sprinkler heads!

The old rainbow sprinkler is great fun in a swimsuit, but it's the most wasteful way to water plants. Too much evaporation.

TOOL LANGUAGE
LANGUAGE TOOLS

If we call a shovel a spade and a bucket a can, what do we call a wagon? What other tool terms will be helpful to learn in the land of gardening D.I.Y.?

Fix your WAGON

I'll pull you, next!

Pulling a wagon makes arms stronger-- but not longer.

Your little brother probably won't mind going for a ride in the Radio Flyer, even after you have used it to haul around your potted starts and dirty digging tools. Your parents will mind the mud on the seat of his pants, however, if he tries to sit down on the couch!

A WHEELBARROW

is ideal for moving and dumping soil from one part of the garden to another.

A set of wheels takes the weight off your back.

A GARDEN CART

has a place for soil, plus sections for pots, gloves and hand tools.

It's good to have a place to set your tools down, so that you don't lose them in the greenery or step on them by accident. You really will get a smack on the nose from the handle of a rake or hoe if you step on its teeth. Tools can also rust if left out.

A BASKET OR TRUG

is a non-wheeled organizer for toting your trowel, gloves, pruners and hand-weeders, but maybe not your snacks.

You can use a 5-gallon pail, accessorized with a handy, multi-pocket pouch insert. Baskets and buckets help you put away your toys!

An APRON with pockets

A SUN HAT

and a cushioned kneeling PAD

As with any hobby or interest, there is seemingly no end to the gadgets you can find available for purchase, but only some of them are truly **essential** to you, the gardener. I would never be found without:

GLOVES

Not only do they protect your hands from slivers and soil microbes, they can keep your rings from getting lost, prevent blisters, and make you feel stronger!

waterproof coating →

breathable top ↓

Make sure you have a little "wiggle room. If your hands tend to get sweaty, you can put a little baby powder inside. Let damp gloves dry in the sun. Never dry your soggy or sweaty gloves in your microwave. (you know who you are, Kevin.) They probably won't melt, but the unique odor will hang around for a few weeks.

TROWEL

The short-handled version of a spade, available in

varying widths. Not sure? Start with something in the middle. My favorite trowel — 20 years and counting — is black polycarbonate with a "here I am" orange handle.

No, it's not a coctail fork or a weenie roaster. This object is an asparagus knife, also known as a dandelion WEEDER. It gets down into narrow spaces and lets you reach those immortal dandelion taproots.

Unless they specify on the label that they can withstand machine washing, try sticking to a gentle rinsing by hand, in the sink.

PRUNER

I am a confessed Prunaholic. There is no garden task I prefer to hand pruning and fine-tuning a woody plant. While it is not a recommended task for the very young, or anyone inclined to run with scissors,

This is a single-blade **bypass** pruner. If you treat it well, it will be your pal for life.

cutting edge →

The handles should fit your hand comfortably, and squeezing them together should not be a struggle. Look for easy "action" and no annoying squeak.

pruning know-how is priceless, and a cheap pruner is worthless. Japanese-made pruners fit my child-sized hands particularly well. They also stay in my back pocket.

A STEP UP

Long-handled pruners, loppers and pole saws are very useful for those fruits, vines and branches that are slightly out of reach. Occasionally, however, you will need just a bit more height (or a professional).

a **cut-and-hold** extended pruner reaches the grapes and the wisteria, which need trimming every week, all summer.

This 2-D wooden ladder leans against a wall or tree and is super shaky. It should stay in those old comedy movies, where it belongs.

4 Legs!

This is a locking **stepladder.** It has sturdy, actual steps, and I can climb to the third one without getting too dizzy.

This is an **orchard** ladder. My grandfather used one to harvest coffee, in Puerto Rico, with his dad and brothers.

CAN YOU TOP THIS?

Top, topper, topping. These words have many pleasant associations. A spinning top is a timeless toy. A top could be your favorite T-shirt, or the highest point on the hill, the pinnacle of your achievements. Up in the tree tops we find the lofty eagle's nest, or your secret clubhouse. But can you Top a tree? All trees are tops in my book, but the only tree that should be topped is the decorated Christmas tree, variety. Happy toppings can be found atop an ice cream sundae, pie à-la-mode, a baked potato or a salad. Unhappy toppings are the sad fate of street trees, whose tops grew up into the telephone wires and electric cables. Hapless tree-toppers, in "cherry picker" truck cranes, buzz cut those tree tops. It is not a pretty sight. We say, **STOP!** You must not TOP!

GOOD TOP

BAD TOP

GOOD TOPPING

TREE TOPPERS TO KNOW

Tree-topping (of the chainsaw persuasion) can lead, in extreme cases, to tree toppling, if rot sets into the dead core wood of the large-diameter leader, or main, upright trunk. The entire tree can hollow out inside and, thus weakened, can be blown over in a storm. Sometimes a tree just needs a little bit off the top to keep it from interfering with the power lines. The best remedy for this is a pruning technique called, "Windowing", which selectively removes entire branches closest to the wires, without tip-cutting.

wires pass through the "window"

↑ leader kept its head

A little bit off the top, please!

BIG TOP BARBER
WALK-INS WELCOME
TIPS, TOO!

A "windowed" willow will still look a bit odd, but no branch tips were cut and it was not topped. Try to avoid planting tall trees under wires.

Now, would you still hire TIP-TOP Tree Service ?

"Poodle", or "Cloud" pruning is a real thing.

BRANCH MANAGEMENT

Pruning is a skill and an art, and also probably the most misunderstood of all gardening tasks. Mis-pruned branches are everywhere, and it is so much easier to begin with correct cuts than to spend the next three years making corrective ones. Here are some basic rules to guide you and save your trees from becoming amputees.

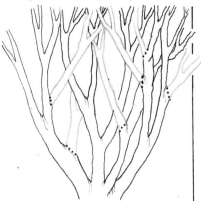

WHEN FACED WITH THIS:
crossing, broken, ingrown and "in the way" branches.

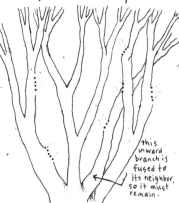

this inward branch is fused to its neighbor, so it must remain.

DO THIS:
remove wayward branches at the base of their growth.

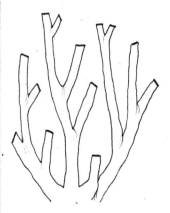

NOT THIS!
what you have now is a coat tree, or a Halloween decoration.

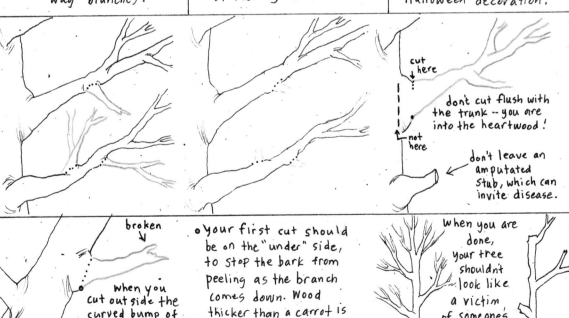

cut here

not here

don't cut flush with the trunk -- you are into the heartwood!

don't leave an amputated stub, which can invite disease.

broken

when you cut outside the curved bump of the "branch collar" the cut can heal.

○ your first cut should be on the "under" side, to stop the bark from peeling as the branch comes down. Wood thicker than a carrot is best removed with a pruning saw, not with a lopper or pruner.

when you are done, your tree shouldn't look like a victim of someone's bad mood or bad taste!

✓   ✗

PRUNELLA

Prunella loved to prune. She was happy to spend hours in the garden, carefully selecting branches that were crowded, broken or growing in toward the center of a tree. To her, it was never a chore. She made the plants look better and live longer, and she didn't care if her sisters called her "Pruney Puss". She kept her tools clean and sharp, and collected up her clippings as she went, so there was never a mess to pick up later on.

Tiarella was impatient. She would lop off great chunks of the plants with the hedge shears, just to be done quickly.

Mitchella was in an even bigger hurry, and fired up the electric chainsaw!

A month later, Prunella's plants still looked great. Her sisters' lopped and chopped branches had all sprouted ugly water spouts and witches' brooms. They decided to pay Prunella their allowance to fix up the mess they had made, and they also stopped calling her "Pruney Puss".

"Water Spouts"

When you cut off the tip of an apple tree branch, dozens of spouts will pop up and reach for the sky.

They are too weak to support fruit, look silly and will resprout every season once a branch has been tip-cut.

← blooms pink!

leaves are a different size!

blooms white!

sucker growth

"Frankentree"

So long, "Suckers"!

Suckers are branches that can spring up from a tree's root system or from the root stock, below the graft line. Ornamental cherry trees are two or three species grafted together. When straight branches shoot up through the weeping top, cut them off!

"Witches' Brooms"

are scary finger-thin thickets that sprout from tip-cut branches.

Tip-cutting used to be done intentionally, to produce lots of wispy wood for weaving baskets. "Pollarding" is the name for this practice.

Unless you are a basket weaver, you have no reason to pollard your innocent tree branches.

If you SAW something, SAY something.

When you amble down the sidewalk and a wild blackberry bramble catches on your clothing or snags your hair, feel free to give it a snip. No one will miss it, and it'll be right back! If a tree branch in the right-of-way tries to poke you in the eye or knock off your wide-brim hat, try knocking on a door and requesting a trim, or offer to come back with a saw to help. Just don't do it like this feller:

Notorious Tree Vandal!

WANTED

fer Crimes aginst Nature

Alias: "El CHOP-O"

He don't take pris'ners

Jus' leaves 'em whar they drop

Don't get in his face-- or he'll cut you down to size!

1. He didn't ask.
2. He tip cut, all over town.
3. He didn't clean up the evidence.

91

A Bad Valentine

"No hay rosas sin espinas," but the thorny issue for this would-be Valentine is a matter of personal taste. This particular Señorita simply detests the combination of red and pink.

Black is the color
    of his true love's hair
But he should have known
    what she would wear.

The lady in Red was not tickled pink.
Red goes with red, not with pink—
        don't you think?

Chapter Seven

Intelligent Garden Design
The Great Landscape

ALL THE COLORS OF THE IRIS

IRIS was a messenger of the Greek gods and the rainbow that linked Earth with other worlds. The colorful part of our eye has been given her name. The flower we call Iris has been used as a symbol throughout history, stylized into an icon carved on the façades of buildings. The flowering, tuberous plant has been grown throughout the temperate zones of the world. But what **color** is an Iris? Science tells us that light bounces off of an object and reflects a particular wavelength of the spectrum into our eyes. Our brains perceive each wave as a specific color. The visible spectrum includes RED, ORANGE, YELLOW, GREEN, BLUE, INDIGO (a deep blue) and VIOLET, and every rainbow is arranged in that order, occasionally repeating the sequence in a second band. Beyond red, and imperceptible to our vision lies INFRARED, and beyond violet there is ULTRAVIOLET, which we can see with special lamps. People who are considered color blind have some difficulty distinguishing between some, but not all colors. Just as plants have been named for people, places, animals, shapes, and nearly everything imaginable, there are flower names we've borrowed to designate specific colors. Do you know:

POPPY   LILAC   SAFFRON   PINK   FUCHSIA   PERIWINKLE

LAVENDER   ORCHID   GOLDENROD   VIOLET ?

Many of these flowers have versions in hues other than their signature ones, too. We also use fruit colors, like CHERRY and KIWI, and leaf colors, like PINE. Paint companies love to borrow from plants when naming their products, as do fabric and cosmetics manufacturers. AVOCADO was once all the rage in appliance enamel!

Iris sibirica, germanica and their kin come in pinks and yellows but this is 'iris'.

The reason Saffron costs so much.

Crocus sativus
Saffron for seasoning and brilliant dye comes from dried stamens.

In need of a nosegay? Lilacs make a most potent bouquet!

Syringa vulgaris
Traditional **lilac** is a pastel purple, but lilacs of any color are fragrant as the purplest prose.

plant these
together
← for the →
ultimate
'bad
Valentine'...

when you plant
every color of
the rainbow
together, you
have made
'a box of
jellybeans'.

Papaver orientale
These poppies won't put
you to sleep. Not in such
a vibrant **poppy** red!

Dianthus caryophyllus
What is more quintessentially
pink than a pink carnation?
Don't forget its smaller cousins,
the cottage pink and clove pink.

Solidaster luteus
Ye olde roadside
goldenrod, blamed
and defamed for
inciting allergies.

Fuchsia hybrida
Fuchsia blooms come in
some strange combinations,
but here is the namesake.

Lavandula spp.
Assorted species of
lavender give us that
famous hue and sachets, too.

Phalaenopsis spp.
'**Orchid** pink' refers
exclusively to the
tint of the Moth
Orchid.

Viola
One of
many
sweet,
shade-
happy
violets
in shades
of
purple.

Primula auricula
If you hear someone
refer to a tint of
yellow as '**primrose**',
they are thinking of
this popular bedding
plant. It was first
called a 'prime rose',
in reference to its
early bloom time.

Baptisia tinctoria
Wild **indigo** is only one
longstanding fabric
dye source from the
pea family. 'Dyer's woad'
is an old-fashioned name
for some of the 'brooms'
and 'waxens' whose petals
yield strong, bright yellows.
But we don't call yellow, woad.

Vinca major
One of several
plants called,
'**periwinkle**',
which is a
distinctive
sorta purple,
sorta blue,
and sorta
muted or dusty.

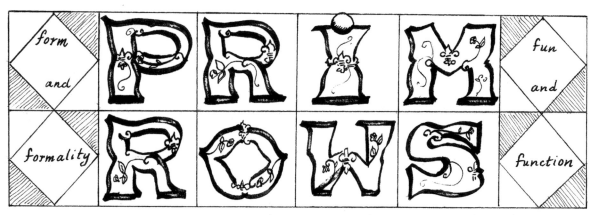

PRIM ROWS

form and formality

fun and function

The style of a garden can reflect the tastes of its owner — who was not in every case its designer — or its particular function. Unless you live in a planned community whose residents agree to keep their lawns manicured and their plant selections traditional, just about anything goes. (You should still try to keep it legal, noninvasive, and avoid hazards to life and limb.) The neighborhood in which I have now spent half my life is very eclectic. That means that the houses, which were built anywhere from one hundred and ten years ago to those currently under construction vary considerably in size and design. The landscapes surrounding them are equally diverse. Even the most neglected yard has at least one gnarled old tree, from a bygone era, or some small plant whose seeds sneaked in and took.

Some gardens begin with a plan, and as with many good intentions, lose the plot over time and changing ownership. One important point to remember is the function of your garden. Are you the proprietor of a Victorian Manor-turned Bed and Breakfast, whose grounds are used to host wedding ceremonies? I imagine not, but in any case, your garden should be a place where you will enjoy spending time, whether or not there is music, dancing, and plenty of cake. Let's take a gander at some of the more recognizable approaches to garden design.

Formal

Formal gardens tend to be very tidy and symmetrical and require enormous, regular upkeep to maintain their neat appearance. They typically feature an assortment of tightly-clipped hedgerows, knot gardens of herbs and blooming bedding plants, a rill or reflecting pool with a fountain, a gazebo for shaded seating and dining, attractive stone paths and patios, some interesting sculptures, and an out-building or two, in which to store tools.

 They afford a peek into the history of European manor homes, if you are a guest (weddings!).

 A nice place to visit, but I wouldn't want to live there (no worries!).

There are no neighbors to even ignore. All plants must behave, and weeds are strictly banished.

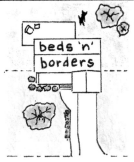

beds 'n' borders

Traditional gardens are what you most often see, in front of all styles of homes. The arrangement of plants is not entirely symmetrical, although plantings tend to be confined to rows and beds along the home's foundation, or lining walkways and fences. There is one medium to large deciduous tree set squarely in the middle of one half of the front lawn, which is most likely planted with sod or turfgrass. There may be a small flowerbed at the base of the tree, or — for the more adventurous — a separate island of plants in the other half.

 It's familiar, it's safe and the lettercarrier doesn't need a machete to get to the mailbox by the front steps.

 Maybe it's a little too familiar? Kids and pet dogs are banished to the backyard. Miss a few mowings and the lawn is full of weeds.

 Neighbors' kids may mow your lawn for five bucks, if they're bored enough.

Cottage garden style began among English 'labouring folk' ~ that's British for poor, working class people — who were allotted a small plot of land upon which to live in a humble, thatch-roofed cottage. They could scratch out their supper of roots and greens and perhaps keep a pig or some chickens. Herbs were a useful thing to have on hand when illness inevitably struck, and flowers lifted the dour mood or could be sold at the market. The only rule for cottage gardening: make use of every available square inch of soil.

Choose plants you like. Choose plants you love. Collect and trade seeds and seedlings with your neighbors. Forgo the lawn, unless you have sheep to graze. Feed bees, butterflies and birds with joyful flowers.

Many weeds are edible. Learn to identify them. Make salad, soup or stirfry.

Native gardens include as many non-imported species as possible. Purists will plant only varieties local to their region. The aim is two-fold. Native plants attract and feed local animals that have lost habitat to our ever-expanding development and paving over of nature. By growing trees and shrubs with a year-round sequence of berries and dried seeds, songbirds will come to visit or take up residence. By including some birdbaths or other water features you can create a true oasis for wildlife. In some locales you can apply for wildlife sanctuary certification, and proudly mount a sign declaring your tiny Eden an honorary wildlife habitat. Enjoy the birdsong!

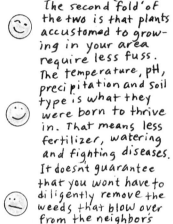

The second 'fold' of the two is that plants accustomed to growing in your area require less fuss. The temperature, pH, precipitation and soil type is what they were born to thrive in. That means less fertilizer, watering and fighting diseases. It doesn't guarantee that you won't have to diligently remove the weeds that blow over from the neighbor's non-native garden.

Rockeries and terraced gardens offer an appealing and necessary solution to the challenge of building and planting on a steep slope. If your house sits on a rise that's thirty feet above street level and you can't afford a private ski lift, you will need some reliable stairs. An uninterrupted course of steps makes for an exhausting climb and a dizzying descent. Terracing introduces stepped garden plateaus all the way up, allowing you to rest at every landing and access your plants without the likelihood of tumbling over.

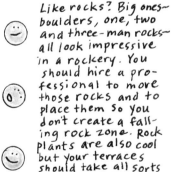

Like rocks? Big ones—boulders, one, two and three-man rocks—all look impressive in a rockery. You should hire a professional to move those rocks and to place them so you don't create a falling rock zone. Rock plants are also cool but your terraces should take all sorts of plant varieties.

Edible gardens are typically built with love and donated materials and funds, by volunteer gardeners who know the happiness people get from plucking and eating fresh produce. Not everyone has the time, energy, space, knowledge or budget to cultivate fresh fruit. An edible garden that is open to the public can share not only the surplus berries, kale, plums, beans, pak choi and grapes but will usually have gardeners willing to teach you and accept your offers to weed.

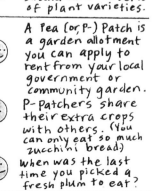

A Pea (or P-) Patch is a garden allotment you can apply to rent from your local government or community garden. P-Patchers share their extra crops with others. (You can only eat so much zucchini bread.) When was the last time you picked a fresh plum to eat?

Zero Scaping

HOW DRY I AM...

When you come across a property with a house plopped roughly in the middle of a patch of dry, dusty ground, an old tree stump with an empty pot on top, a few clumps of weedy grass and a struggling, neglected shrub, you have found a classic example of zero·scaping, or the virtual lack of a landscape. Surely a few green signs of life would cheer the place up and help the house stop looking as though it dropped there from the sky only to become abandoned. A garden doesn't have to be high-maintenance. It doesn't have to require huge amounts of water, either. Not if you learn the secrets of:

Xeriscaping

The word, from the Greek xeri, which means dry, was coined in 1981 by an environmental planner for the Denver, Colorado Water Department. Denver's summers tend to be hot and dry, and most popular landscaping plants have a stressful time once June arrives. Xeriscaping is a water-conserving plan that approaches long-term gardening success using eight basic principles.

1. **Plan and design.** Group plants together based on their sun or shade preferences, water needs and native soil type.

2. **Practical turf.** Less lawn is better lawn.

3. **Right plants.** You don't have to limit your pallette to succulents, oatgrass and yucca, but if your rockery faces south or west, it wouldn't be wise to plant any Japanese maples or blueberry bushes.

4. **Improve soil.** Work in some compost. Organic matter helps hold onto moisture.

5. **Mulch.** A top-dressing of something ~ more compost, wood chips, nut shells ~ cuts down on evaporation.

6. **Irrigate wisely.** Soaker hoses and drip systems deliver water to roots, not leaves.

7. **Catch rain.** Barrels capture runoff via your gutter downspouts and store it for later.

8. **Proper maintenance.** Turn out those thirsty, freeloading weeds. Avoid over fertilizing.

Plants for your Xeriscape are not necessarily limited to cacti, Sedum and Sage. There is a generous range of less thirsty species, from shrubs to creepers, and since they will require little water, you can concentrate on irrigating a couple of trees. Most trees become less dependent upon the garden hose after their roots have had three years of being encouraged to reach down below by your regular, **deep** watering. A tiny sprinkle every day keeps the roots near the surface, waiting for you to show up with your watering can, so get out there with the hose twice a week and give them a good soaking!

Replace the builders' sad, brown Junipers and Arborvitae with Hebe, Azara and Coprosma. Shrub Euonymus is heavily used in public settings, but it is a sturdy citizen, and makes a reliable, drought-resistant hedge or backdrop.

Here is an eclectic assortment of plants that can thrive on near neglect, in no particular order and with a generous display of colorful blooms included.

Papaver (Poppy)
Poppies come in annual and perennial species and are easy from seed.

Centranthus (Jupiter's Beard/Red Valerian)
This plant can grow in dust. It will pop up, blooming its heart out, through a crack in a concrete wall. If there is too much of it ~ or if it springs up through your driveway ~ simply pluck it out. Its roots are shallow.

Agastache (Hyssop)
This is not the true herbal Hyssop, but it comes in fascinating, indescribable colors, with the additional novelty of scents mimicking licorice, root beer and 7-Up°.

Dianthus (Pinks, carnations, Sweet William)

Veronica (Speedwell, Hebe)
Hebe is the shrubbier version, but every veronica bears dainty white, pink or purple flowers above a surprising assortment of leaf shapes and sizes.

Salvia (Sage)
Give this one space, as it can get quite big. Smells great.

Liatris (Blazing Star)
An exploding feather of delicate petals.

Penstemon (Beardtongue)
Versatile, beautiful and long-lived. Think of it as a more serious snapdragon.

Nepeta (Catmint)
This genus includes catnip, but all are mints with aromatic leaves and delicate little flowers.

Perovskia (Russian Sage)
Not edible—unless you're a bee, and this plant is a feast for honey bees in late summer, who flock to its clouds of purple.

Helianthemum (Sunrose)
If I had to choose only one blooming, evergreen creeper, it would likely be this one. It blooms in so many pretty colors, and even the leaves vary from chalky blue to deep green. They last forever.

Cistus (Rock rose)
Not a rose. Larger version of Sun rose – which isn't a rose either. Some have aromatic leaves.

Ceanothus (California Lilac)
Not a Lilac (good, if you are allergic to those). Comes in shrub or in creeping form, both of which attract bees and compliments with their shocks of electric blue-violet flowers.

Stachys (Lamb's ear)
Eminently pettable, soft fuzzy leaves and sweet little pink blooms.

Nigella (Love-in-a-mist)
A whimsical, self-re-seeding annual with unusual dried pods.

Knautia (Red Scabiosa)
Plant one and you will, happily, have it for life.

Delospermum (Ice plant)
Neon-bright petals on creeping, crispy succulent stems. Juicy leaves I loved to snap as a kid (shhh!).

Campanula (Hare bell)
Also called blue bells, as some bloom in shades of blue. So many to choose from, and all of them are easy~breezy.

dream GARDEN time

Clouds decorate the skyscape in hypnotic and constantly changing patterns. There is no plan to the daytime sky. Only the stars inhabit fixed positions within their particular home constellations, appearing to travel across the night sky as we observe them from our revolving planet. There is an awful lot of space out there in Space, but down here on Earth, where we go about our daily activities, we have a finite amount of room. When it comes to creating a garden it's good to formulate a plan, so you can make the best use of your available space.

Winter is a great time to thumb through gardening magazines or scroll through websites and make notes of plants that catch your eye. You can research them to see if they are hardy in your own climate. Some nurseries stay open year round to offer winter plants and ideas.

A Garden plan helps you avoid such mistakes as shading out your entire vegetable patch with a giant elderberry bush or surrendering your front walkway to a sea of creeping geraniums.

Think about each plant's sun O, shade ● or partial ◑ requirements. Will it keep its leaves all year or be bare twigs through the winter? Will it need extra water?

You can measure your entire yard or just one area and plot it on graph paper to see what will fit.

You can organize the list of plants you like into categories, based on their expected mature size, so you don't end up planting a ten-foot wide tree three feet from your picture window or a two-foot tall subshrub down behind a rock wall where no one will ever see it.

BIG TREES: Taller than twelve feet by their tenth year of growth and at least six feet wide. The trees that will provide you shade are the backbone of any garden's design.

- Shadow zone.

SMALL to MEDIUM TREES and SHRUBS: It is more practical and easier to plant anything with a substantial root ball before settling in all of the bedding plants and pavers.

Remember me?

PERENNIALS: Even your small, flowering plants benefit from some fore-thought. Knowing their potential sizes helps you prevent shorter plants from disappearing behind taller ones and tells you how far apart to space them so they won't compete.

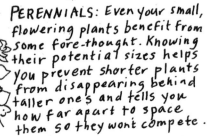

The graph paper has a 1/4" grid. ☐ Pretend that each 1/4" box on the grid represents one square foot of your garden area. Leave your trees some room to grow, but remember that they don't all get to the same height. A 6-foot tall tree that is 6-foot wide can grow partially beneath the canopy of a taller tree, like so :

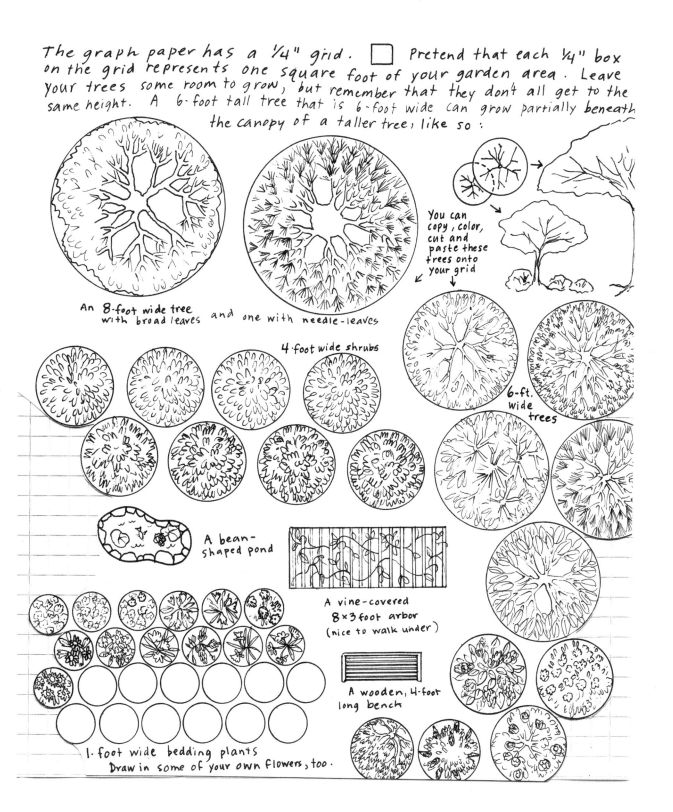

You can copy, color, cut and paste these trees onto your grid

An 8-foot wide tree with broad leaves and one with needle-leaves

4-foot wide shrubs

6-ft. wide trees

A bean-shaped pond

A vine-covered 8×3 foot arbor (nice to walk under)

A wooden, 4-foot long bench

1-foot wide bedding plants Draw in some of your own flowers, too.

It's a Long Way to TOPIARY

CLIP CLIP

SNAP SNAP

BUZZ BUZZ

SNIP SNIP

NIP NIP

LOP LOP

CHOP CHOP

Topiary is the practice of sculpting trees and shrubs into unusual shapes. Balls, cubes, ovals and cones are not unusual in themselves, and there are indeed some plants whose growth is naturally so dense and symmetrical that they appear to have been trimmed with hedge shears. To shear is to tip-cut the end — that terminal, apical bud ~ of every branch in sight. Shearing creates a thick privacy screen and a tidy green border for defining property lines and separating garden areas. Hedges also make effective mazes. A maze doubles back on itself and loops around, creating a long path that takes up a smaller footprint than one which is laid out in a straight line. A meditative maze can simply be a line you follow on the ground. A trickier maze will have dead ends and walls you can't see over. In the maze above are the tools Edgar Clipperhands needs to collect up. Please help him make his way through without crossing back over his own steps. He has more box woods to carve up before lunch time and hollies to hack before dinner...

Topiary hedges can be formal or fun — or both at once. There is a cemetery in my neighborhood whose front entrance is lined with enormous green gumdrops. There are no beasts with leafy faces, but that motif is popular in certain theme parks and in at least one very scary novel by Stephen King. If you find yourself being chased by a large, verdant lion I hope you have remembered to bring along a pair of trusty pruners or a versatile chaperone like Edgar Clipperhands.

GUMDROPS AND LOLLIPOPS LEND A BIZARRE SENSE OF WHIMSY FOR THE DEARLY DEPARTED AND ENSURE ONGOING EMPLOYMENT FOR THE LIVING.

Once you have sheared your shrubs into fun shapes they will never look natural again, so make sure you know what you're getting yourself into. If you've simply hip-hop-gotta-chop-can't-stop, you'll be set for life! If you'd rather let your plants do their own thang but you'd still really, really like to start your own hedge menagerie, there is a kinder approach to sculpting your verdant zoo. A topiary frame is a wire armature, constructed of chicken wire or other bendable, galvanized fence cloth. A wire skeleton is packed with dampened sphagnum moss and peaty soil. Sedum or vines — typically Ivy — are rooted into the moss, covering the frame until it resembles a green deer, Labrador Retriever, frog or Yeti. (The resemblance will vary with your sculpting abilities and willingness to suspend disbelief.) You can also stick with the moss alone, spraying it with water to keep it green or leaving it to dry into a more convincing doe-y, Sasquatch brown. Some people, like my friend Harris have a genuine knack for creating moss beasts. You can always start with cones!

Rosemary is a small-leaved evergreen herb whose shrubby branches lend themselves well to clipping. Another plus to shaping Rosemary is that it smells wonderful when cut, something which cannot be said of Boxwood. Rosemary is delicious cooked into stews and on roasts. Boxwood attracts cats and dogs. Most dwarf Hebe (a shrubby Veronica that blooms in summer) can also be gumdropped without too much trouble. A shrub honeysuckle, Lonicera nitida (non-edible) makes a good topiary subject, but be aware that this plant likes to spread by root suckers, so you could end up with a thicket of them. As for mazes, you can create a miniature labyrinth using smaller herbs like Thyme. You can also make quilt-like patterns or spell out simple words using low bedding plants with contrasting leaf and flower colors. That makes for a fun summer project and needs few tools.

Gone, but not fergotten.

Say it:

"Don't spray it!"

Chapter Eight

Plant. Eat. Repeat.

Organic Food from Your Garden

Smallfarm   BIG PHARM

The *Old Farmers Almanac* is a long-running publication filled with helpful charts to guide your planting selections and timing. It will teach you about companion plants and crop rotation, old-style.

to many people, the word **garden** means vegetables. Home veggie gardening reaches back to a time when most families filled their stewpots with produce grown on a small patch outside their humble abode. They kept a couple of chickens for protein from the eggs, and perhaps traded the occasional hen for some mutton from a neighbor who raised sheep.

Someone discovered that a squirt of tobacco juice kept marauding insects off the lettuce. Fertilizer came from manure provided by those chickens and from other barnyard animals. Any weeds were removed by hand, often ending up in the soup of the day. Dedicated farmers worked long hours, against the elements, to raise crops others would be willing to purchase.

Host a Roots-Rock Reggae Party! Your healthy soil should be jumpin' with insect activity and good microbes.

You da bees' knees

Good grub!

as life became more industrialized and increasing numbers of people moved into cities to live and work, farming evolved into the mechanized, corporatized, chemically-driven agriculture that keeps most of the world's people fed. **Agriscience** has developed hardier cultivars with higher crop yields and greater disease resistance. The result is that food supplies on the planet are less scarce, although surplus produce doesn't always reach the tables of some of the world's hungriest populations, without the help of aid organizations and charitable donations. Big agriculture is big business.

Organic pest management approaches insects and diseases with products using lightweight oils and targeted natural bacteria. peaches, apples, bell peppers, grapes, strawberries and cherries, lettuce, celery, spinach, nectarines and potatoes tend to be the commercially-grown produce most heavily treated. They carry pesticide residues. Try to buy these from organic growers, if you can.

Another unfortunate by-product of agricultural development is the early decades of pesticide experimentation. The concept of "Better Living Through Chemistry" went hand-in-hand with the mid twentieth century's efforts to concoct more effective weapons of war, some of them chemical.

Non-military industrial chemistry also brought such random revelations as the fact that ethoxyquin, a compound added to rubber during the manufacturing process, killed grain weevils. Eureka! Animal feed stored alongside some farmer's tractor tires was free of critters, so ethoxyquin became one of the many unnatural elixirs added to the food supply. How many pesticides do you spray in your garden? If you are growing plants **organically**, the answer to that question should be few to none at all.

2 cups flour
1 cup flowers

Some people don't mind eating the same exact thing, day after day...

An Aahh-Baloney Sammitch for lunch.

ptthhlthhh

Scream-O-wheat for breakfast.

why is it always me?!

Meat mope for dinner, with smashed potatoes.

hic

ho-hum. "Blue Plate Special" my eye.

BUT,

throughout human history most people have become excited whenever someone took a chance and introduced something new into the daily menu. Often these novel introductions underwent a round or two of risky test-tasting. Word-of-mouth ~also known as folk wisdom~ generally prevented repeated loss of life, when the experimental food proved less than healthful. When you are hungry enough you will eat just about anything, but our bodies cannot process everything. We'll leave that to the goats and the buzzards. It's important to ask questions before you sample random plants you see while out adventuring. Some of the prettiest, translucent red berries belong to the *Deadly Nightshade*!

Um- 'scuse me...

Yowch!! **W**hich is pokier — Pokeweed (Phytolacca) or the pokey, pokey artichokey (Cynara)? Both will cause you serious stomach consequences, should you eat them raw. When you prepare an artichoke, you are cooking the flower bud of a giant thistle. Various thistles and their seeds are valued as food and as cleansing detoxifiers. The same prickly crystals that clean your inner workings— particularly a congested liver ~ can bring on a miserable bellyache if you don't prepare them properly. Pokeweed berries contain poisonous seeds that have medicinal value in treating pain and inflammation, an ironic counterpoint to the pain that could result from ingesting the plant! My friend, Thad grew up in Arkansas eating his grandma's *poke salad*. After she'd boiled and rinsed it at least three times it was apparently safe to ingest, as Thad grew up to attest.

More delicate —and less prickly —flowers are the darlings of the gourmets' kitchen. Magazines, restaurants and wedding cake bakers adore their decorative and flavorful qualities, and so can you. Flowers can make a salad prettier. You can bake them into cookies or float them in your lemonade. Make sure to research which species are edible, and unless you have grown them yourself, ask whether they have been sprayed by whoever tends the yard where they grow.

YOUNG DANDELION FLOWERS TASTE LIKE HONEY.

NASTURTIUM FLOWERS ARE SPICY, LIKE PEPPER.

VIOLETS ARE SWEET, CANDIED OR NOT.

LIVING COLOR WHEEL

*C*olor up your calories! Become a colorful character!

Radishes are such a beautiful, jewel-toned root on the exterior. They surprise the unsuspecting with their crisp, bright white interior. Oh- and their often fiery taste!

If you don't care for the taste of beet root, try some cooked beet greens. I prefer them to spinach or kale, but I eat all my greens (and I grew up to be five feet tall !!!)

Eggplant can taste bitter if you don't add the right seasoning. Try some Baba Ghannoush - a yummy eggplant and garlic dip, which is more grey than blue-violet (close your eyes and open your mouth). Never had a blue potato? They taste a lot like a white, red or yellow potato!

A classic tomato is bright red, but tomatoes come in a range of colors, from yellow through a brownish-purple that is almost black. A green tomato has not yet ripened, but it can still be fried and eaten. Peppers and carrots also grow in other colors. Cut up and served all together, they make meals prettier. Some squash fruits have white, tan or green skin, but they are still yellow or orange inside.

Corn comes in lots of colors, too. Blue tortilla chips are made from blue corn. The most interesting cobs are the multicolored Indian corn.

Asparagus is a weird vegetable in a weird color with a weird odor. I am in the "love it" camp, but it is definitely an outlier and perhaps an acquired taste. (Try it again as an adult)

RED
RED-VIOLET
RED-ORANGE
VIOLET
ORANGE
BLUE-VIOLET
YELLOW-ORANGE
BLUE
YELLOW
BLUE-GREEN
YELLOW-GREEN
GREEN

The color wheel is an art tool that displays the rainbow (or, the visible color spectrum) as a circle. In the world of pigments, red, yellow and blue are primary colors — you can't mix two or more other paints together to make these three. Secondary colors are a blend of two primaries (red + yellow = orange). A primary mixed with a secondary makes a tertiary color (red + orange = red-orange). Colors that line up opposite one another are called complementary colors (red/green, violet/yellow). The complements look good next to eachother but if you blend them as paint you get mud. You can paint with vegetable inks or just mix all the colors in your tummy.

Animal, vegetable or mineral? That used to be the first thing you asked when playing "20 Questions". Today, the distinctions are a little less clear, as genetic modification seeks to enhance the characteristics of our produce through the introduction of animal DNA. Technically, scientists have imitated the amino acid sequence that keeps fish alive in freezing waters in order to produce a tomato that could ship without cold damage. This attempt led to the "fishwives' tale" about a tomato that could swim, or something equally silly. A true tomato tale is this one: although it is biologically a fruit, as it forms from a fertilized flower and contains seeds, a tomato is legally now a vegetable, at least in the U.S.A. Taxation makes the government go 'round, and the U.S. Supreme Court put a new spin on tomato imports. It seems that imported fruit was not subject to tariffs in 1893, therefore the growing popularity of tomatoes made them more attractive as taxable vegetables!

Other fruits masquerading in our minds as veggies are the squashes, peppers, and my all-time favorite, the avocado. Those seeds and pits render these sneaky casserole, stew and salad components as the reproductive portion of the plant. Referring back to our initial "20 Questions" question, a fruit is still **vegetable** in nature, as it is not animal (not even a **chick**pea) or mineral (not **stone** fruit).

Vegetable — and fruit — pigments are beneficial to our health. The blue in blueberry skins (xanthocyanins) and the yellow-orange in carrots (carotene) protect our tissues. Anti-oxidants found naturally in produce (foods that grow on trees, shrubs and vines, or sprout directly from the soil) preserve our cells. Unless you are strictly a **vegan** (eating no animal products of any kind) or a **vegetarian** (limiting animal foods in the diet to eggs, fish and dairy) chances are high that you are not consuming the recommended number of daily fruit and veg servings. Produce is expensive because of the labor it takes to grow and harvest food crops. Shipping is not free, either. Any food you can grow for yourself will still cost you in time, effort and water, but when you pick your own strawberries or pluck your own cucumber, not only will it seem like free food, it will taste as fresh as only a fresh-picked fruit — or veggie — can.

Too much of a good thing ... My friend Eva loves the color green. When she talks about green her eyes get big like a kitty's eyes in an anime meme. Eva also loves veggies, and was the first vegan I knew. One week she ate two entire bags of large carrots. I don't know what else she ate that week, but by Friday she wasn't feeling too well, and her skin was glowing yellow from the carotene! The doctor told her that excessive amounts of Vitamin A could harm her liver. After that, Eva made sure to mix up her colors, adding some purples and reds and of course her favorite, green. What is your favorite color? What is your favorite vegetable? Is there any resemblance between the two? Is there a food you run away from because of its color?

EH- WHAT'S UP, DOC?

wax bean

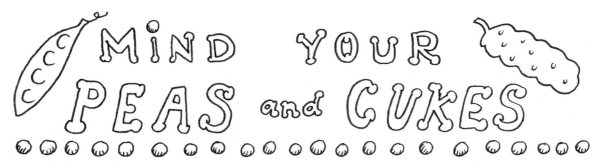

MIND YOUR PEAS and CUKES

Some vegetables grow like weeds. Some vegetables are weeds (dandelion greens, purslane, chick weed, miner's lettuce). Most children grow like weeds, if they eat their vegetables or not. Some children actually like to eat vegetables and will even ask for seconds. Which group includes you? Are there one or two veggies you adore but others you won't dare to try? Peas tend to be a love 'em or leave 'em veg, but if you love peas, the part of the plant you are savoring is its seed. If you open up a packet of seed peas to plant in your pea patch, what you will find is a wrinkled up, dried version of the peas you may have pushed to the edge of your dinner plate. That's if you are accustomed to being served

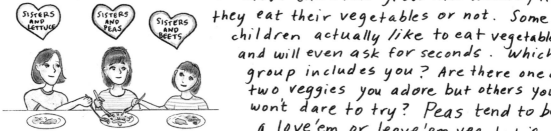

I WAS THE MIDDLE CHILD. AT DINNER TIME, FROM MY LEFT CAME EVERYTHING BUT CARROTS, CORN AND BEETS. FROM MY RIGHT CAME ALL PEAS AND BEANS. I THINK THE DISAPPOINTMENT IN CANNED ZUCCHINI WAS UNIVERSAL. BOTH SISTERS GREW UP TO BE AVERAGE-TO-TALL. WERE THEY RIGHT ABOUT THE LIMA BEANS?

'English Garden Peas', French 'Petits Pois' or, generically speaking, 'shelling peas'. They have been a staple addition to countless pot-pies, stews and soups for centuries. Every ten years or so I will purchase a can of 'Early Peas' out of some odd sense of nostalgia — or because I've forgotten that the canned peas I ate as a young child were truly not the best peas I have ever tasted. They were, however, not the worst. That dubious honor goes to the mushy peas I ate once-is-enough while visiting in England. Feel free to take my word for it.

'MANGE TOUT' IS FRENCH FOR "EAT IT ALL"

SUGAR SNAP PEAS ARE EATEN POD AND ALL.

SNOW PEA PODS ARE FLAT AND FEATURE IN CHINESE CUISINE

YOU POP OPEN THE POD, COLLECT THE COZY LITTLE PEAS IN A BOWL AND COMPOST THE EMPTY POD, OR 'SHELL'.

Frozen peas stay crisp and Eva-approved, glorious green. Fresh peas can be eaten raw or cooked. Sugar-snap peas from my garden don't even make it into the house. They serve as a pick-me-up snack while I'm working outdoors, and my doggie enjoys them, too. I don't know if I've convinced you to give peas a chance, but I don't know of any person who has turned green from eating peas. Try one — they're so little!

Besides peas and their fellow legumes, the beans, other seeds we eat are **pepitas** (toasted pumpkin seeds), sunflower kernels, pignoli (pine nuts) and all sorts of tree nuts (almonds, cashews, pecans, walnuts, macadamia nuts and Brazil nuts). Peanuts are also legumes. Corn kernels are seeds covered in juicy packets lined up in neat rows along the cob. We remove seeds before serving peppers, but thousands of other seeds sneak their way into our meals, barely noticed, inside cucumbers, eggplants, zucchini and tomatoes. Have you ever cut open a bell pepper and been surprised to find a second, smaller pepper growing inside it?

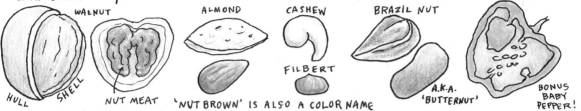

WALNUT — HULL — SHELL — NUT MEAT
ALMOND — 'NUT BROWN' IS ALSO A COLOR NAME
CASHEW — FILBERT
BRAZIL NUT — A.K.A. 'BUTTERNUT'
BONUS BABY PEPPER!

Food safety is a fairly modern topic. When food manufacturing and packaging was a young industry, warehouses were rarely inspected and all manner of unappetizing and —literally— sickening things ended up being swept from the factory floor or falling into vats and joining food-stuffs inside cans and jars. I still remember the story we were told in sixth grade about some of the things that were found in pickle jars besides cucumbers and pickling spices. Factory inspection is a routine requirement now, and foodborne illness rarely comes from cans, jars or frozen packages. Fresh produce can carry some serious hazards, though, and frequent recalls of raw salad mixes, for example, are scary because we can't kill the bacteria on them by cooking thoroughly. Always make sure to remove any slimy leaves and soak, rinse or scrub the other vegetable parts we eat, especially if they will be served without cooking.

LEAVES
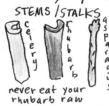
·lettuce ·cabbage ·spinach ·collards ·parsley ·mustard; kale ~ all of those "greens"

STEMS/STALKS

celery rhubarb asparagus
never eat your rhubarb raw

FLOWERS

· broccoli ·cauliflower · squash blossoms

BULBS/ROOTS/TUBERS
·onion ·turnip ·carrot ·rutabaga ·parsnip ·potato ·yam ·taro ·beet

Allergies, intolerance and food sensitivity comprise another, more recent area of dietary awareness. Fruits and vegetables are a vital nutritional resource for our bodies, and there are so many to choose from that even a picky eater can find a few to enjoy. Sometimes a food that is optimal for most people can cause an uncomfortable or even dangerous reaction in a few individuals. Some foods, due to their chemical makeup or accompanying bacteria and fungi fall into a recognized category of high allergen triggers. You probably know someone who has to avoid peanuts, for example. Gluten, which food engineering methods have exaggerated in U.S.-grown wheat, is difficult to digest and causes inflammation in the digestive tract of anyone sensitive to certain proteins. Strawberries, potatoes, eggplant and rhubarb contain a lot of oxalic acid, which can form irritating crystals. My friend, Jo was raised on her dad's peach farm. Not only was Jo allergic to the fuzz on the peaches she helped pick, she would risk canker sores to eat the tomatoes she adored. Jo is also too well-loved by bees, and must carry an Epi-pen wherever she goes!

SPICE TRAVEL

Pepper was our second dog. She arrived at the shelter with that name, which suited her peppy attitude, at the respectable age of eight years. We didn't know where she came from, why she had been surrendered, or what became of her leg (she only had three). Being a 'tripod' didn't seem to slow Pepper down at all. She loved to travel, by car and on paw. Her most amusing feature was her grin ~ two rows of perfectly aligned white teeth. She buried biscuits using her nose.

PEPPER, A DOG WORTH HER SALT.

Pepper knew she was not allowed on the sofa. One afternoon she was having such a good snooze that she didn't hear me come in the door from work. I walked into the front room and there she was, with a guilty look, quickly hopping down to the floor. She launched into a series of welcome home sneezes, displaying that hilarious grin. If she ever napped on the furniture again she managed to keep it a secret.

Pepper, the spice is so common in our world today that we rarely give it much thought. Every salt shaker is partnered with a pepper shaker, although even salt was once a rare commodity. The word **salary** derives from the Latin **salarium**, a reminder that Roman soldiers were paid in salt! For us, even at fast-food restaurants, where food is already loaded with sodium, there is an array of flavorful, free condiments to further enhance the meal. We take for granted all of that

KETCHUP · MUSTARD · VINEGAR · SOY SAUCE · BROWN SAUCE · HOT SAUCE · WORCESTERSHIRE SAUCE · BBQ SAUCE · RANCH DIP... and toss away far too many single-serving, tear-open packets of ketchup, mustard and mayonnaise for take-out.

Salt is an important ingredient for food preservation, and salted, smoked and dried fish and meats kept plenty of people supplied with safe protein sources throughout travel and migration, or at any time that hunting was not possible. Unless you lived surrounded by snow, there was no such thing as refrigeration ~ the electrically-generated kind ~ and perishable foods spoiled quickly. The piquant flavors of pepper and other spices helped to mask the bad taste of rotting meat, even if it may have meant you were sitting down to a bellyache ~ or your final meal.

Spices and the plants they come from tend to originate in tropical places. Seasoning sources include many varied plant parts, from seeds and leaves to roots and flower stamens. The plants themselves are not all related, although the mint family provides many of the herbs whose leaves we've all tasted. Mints don't require tropical heat to grow, and the seasoning they yield doesn't approach the hot sensation that most tropical flavorings produce on your tongue, either. Once people from the "West" (Europe) discovered the spice markets of the "East" (India, China and various islands, as well as parts of Africa and the Middle East), trade routes were established to keep a steady supply arriving to their stewpots. Before Italy was a unified country, Genoa and Venice had become large, prosperous city-states because they had a monopoly on the spice trade. Travel over land to reach the Orient was long, and necessitated passing through too many countries and borders. Ships from Europe could make a time-consuming and tedious voyage all the way around the African continent to get to the spice markets. In 1485, Columbus approached Spain's king and queen

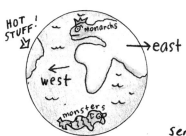

to seek their backing for his seemingly crazy idea of sailing westward across the Atlantic ocean as a 'short-cut' to Japan. He had already been turned down by the king of Portugal, where he'd been residing. It took until 1492 ~ when Spain's Fernando and Isabel had unified their kingdoms to their satisfaction and consolidated Catholic rule ~ for them to approve the dubious plans of Columbus and see him off in three semi-seaworthy vessels. His calculations of the distance were off, but more critically, none of the mariners or mapmakers who had advised him seemed to be aware of the existence of another two enormous continents located between the "east" and the "west". World history was completely altered, forever, by the alleged quest to obtain some seasoning!

The 'pepper' that Columbus encountered in the "West Indies" is of the juicy, nightshade variety. These and their tomato and potato relatives were all carried back to a very surprised Europe, where they remain a staple.

Red, yellow and green 'CHILI PEPPERS' — botanically, **Capsicum annuum**

For some people, the hotter the better, even if they look like they are suffering through their meal. What about you? How many ☆ stars ☆ do you like?

Black pepper, meanwhile, comes from grinding the dried, pea-sized berry of the **Piper nigrum** plant, native to hot places such as Indonesia. It is a climbing shrub that grows up to 12 feet tall. The United States buys more than 25,000 **tons** of peppercorns a year. To produce white pepper, the corns of the same plant are handled and dried differently.

PEPPER'S FLAVOR COMES FROM AN ACRID RESIN AND OIL IT CONTAINS.

I DON'T CARE FOR THE FLAVOR OF PEPPER, AND AM ALWAYS PREPARED FOR THE LOOK OF DIS-APPOINTMENT ON THE

—I'LL PASS, THANKS—

FACE OF THE RESTAURANT SERVER, WHOSE ONE SMALL JOY IN LIFE SEEMS TO BE THE OPPORTUNITY TO GRIND FRESH PEPPER ONTO SALAD.

meloncauliflower

if your world seems dry and dismal and t.v. sitcom melodrama is about to drive you out of your gourd, perhaps it's time to see how the juicy half live. Let's tune into a fresh episode of ... ... a wholesome peek into the lives of the vitamin C rich.

'Meet the Crenshaws'

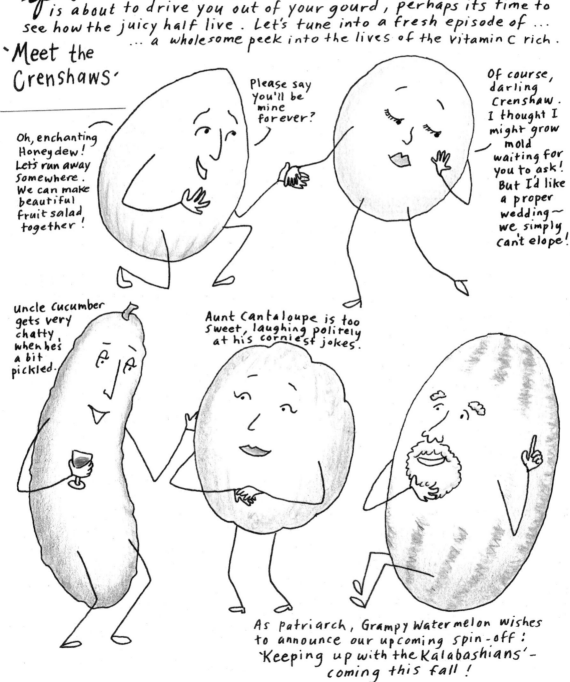

Oh, enchanting Honeydew! Let's run away somewhere. We can make beautiful fruit salad together!

Please say you'll be mine forever?

Of course, darling Crenshaw. I thought I might grow mold waiting for you to ask! But I'd like a proper wedding — we simply can't elope!

uncle Cucumber gets very chatty when he's a bit pickled.

Aunt Cantaloupe is too sweet, laughing politely at his corniest jokes.

As patriarch, Grampy Watermelon wishes to announce our upcoming spin-off: 'Keeping up with the Kalabashians' — coming this fall!

# of cabbages and kin

Kale, kale, the gang's all here! Meet yet another veggie family — Cruciferae, the mustard family. (You could also call it the cabbage family. I don't know how mustard got top billing.) I grew up eating cooked corned beef and cabbage, not realizing that the crunchy summer treat I enjoyed as 'cole slaw' derived from the very same plant. Cabbage is also known as a **cole** crop, and when boiled for hours in the traditional St. Paddy's Day stew ~ or pickled into sauerkraut ~ transforms into a mushy, semi-transparent, gassy glop. **Brassicas**, who count among their numbers broccoli, cauliflower and romanescu, often get a bad rap, as feared and detested by some as they are loved and respected by others. In spite of their mixed reception, they were some of the earliest crops to be cultivated by ancient agriculturalists.

Mighty Kale, the founding father, or the mother of all things cabbage. I first met this one in my college dining hall, boiled and chopped, but later grew it and grew to enjoy it stir-fried or sautéed. A little lemon tahini dressing cooked in counters the bitter notes associated with many of the highly alkaline brassicas.

Shy Cauliflower, so long hidden under a generous coating of cheddar cheese sauce. Who would have guessed that she'd emerge from obscurity to take center stage as an exciting, gluten-free pizza crust? Cauliflower, as it turns out, turns into an excellent grain-free flour. Its naturally bland ~ some would say blah ~ flavor and understated pigmentation (it didn't make the color wheel) help it fly under the radar.

Rockin' Broccoli, the unequivocal friend or foe. You will either take to this one and put it in everything, or swear off the stuff for life. But before you run a mile, try some broccoli stalk coleslaw.

King Cole, the cabbage. Valued through the ages for its vitamin C content, a feature it shares with its other crucifer cousins, which include Turnip (you can eat the root **and** the greens), Brussels Sprouts (you can eat them ~ I'd rather not...), Napa (or Chinese cabbage) and my friend Connie's fave, Kohlrabi.

I HATE YOUR GUTS!

I LOVE YOUR GUTS!

The commendable Crucifers are high in anti-oxidants, which fight cancer-causing free radicals in the human colon ~ known as your gut. Even if your inner child rebels against eating its vegetables, your inner innards will receive them gladly.

A CLOVE A DAY KEEPS THE VAMPIRES AWAY

I heard it improved blood circulation.

I heard it lowered blood pressure.

I couldn't say whether or not the ancient Egyptians believed in vampires, but they were familiar with garlic's health-promoting properties. Tutankhamen made sure to take some bulbs along for his future reign in the afterlife. When the Boy King's elaborate tomb was uncovered, garlic was included among the various foods deemed essential to the living. Did it offend — or fend-off — evil spirits? Garlic has made other historical appearances, most of which did not have to wait thousands of years to be revealed. Medical mentions include:

references in ancient Babylonian texts tout the plant's help in curing many infectious diseases.

ninth century Japanese physicians established a garlic sanitorium, where garlic was administered to treat patients with infections.

during the 1665 Great Plague of London, garlic was used to ward off contagion (not vampires). I don't know whether the wary ingested it or wore it, dried, around the neck...

yet another epidemic ~ this time of cholera, in 1866 ~ saw people eating large amounts of garlic to stave off infection.

renowned French physician, Louis Pasteur, described garlic's antibacterial capabilities in the mid 1800s.

used during WWI to treat intestinal infections in soldiers.

Rock, paper, scissors... garlic? Garlic beats them all, and it does repel mosquitoes ~ those real-life vampires!

Like potatoes, garlic isn't grown from seed. You can save a clove or two to grow a new head ~ of garlic, of course.

He likes to keep cool...

but also dry, so he best be chillin' on the kitchen countertop

There is such a thing as a garlic pill.

"GAR-LIKE"

It is designed for medicinal use, not for cooking, and claims to be "odor-free"...

HEAD

CLOVE

Garlic originally grew in Central Asia, where excellence in Asian cuisine also originally grew.

Botanically, garlic is known as **Allium sativa**. It is a bulb, related to leeks, onions, and such ornamentals as the Belladonna Lily, a.k.a. Amaryllis, this last one being toxic!!

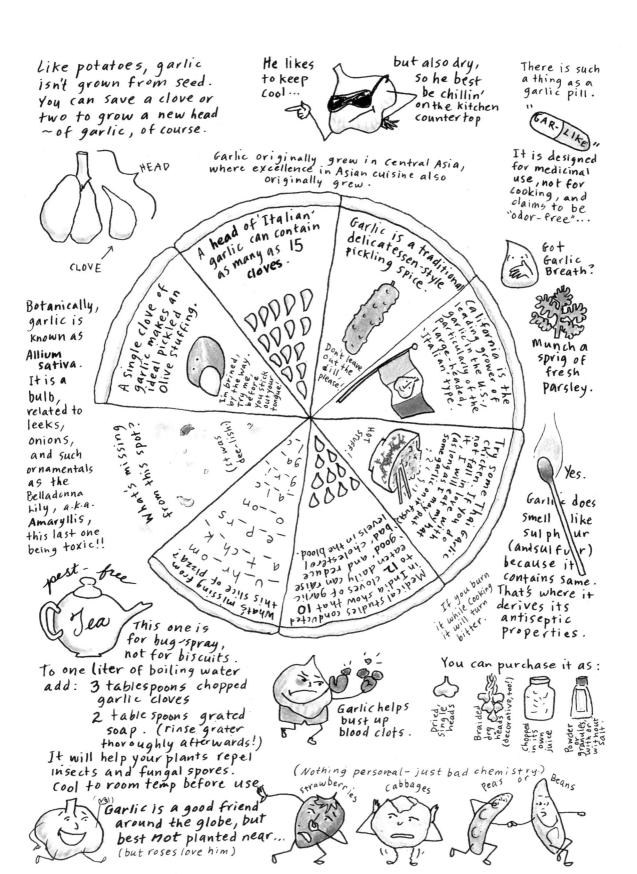

A head of 'Italian' garlic can contain as many as 15 cloves.

Garlic is a traditional delicatessen-style pickling spice.

California is the leading grower of the U.S.! I will love it, I will love my hot some garlic or not. (as long as I eat a large-headed, 'Italian' type.

Got Garlic Breath?

Munch a sprig of fresh parsley.

A single clove of garlic makes an ideal pickled olive stuffing.

In brined by the way, try me before you stick out your tongue!

Don't leave out the dill, please!

Try some Thai garlic

Hot stuff!

Yes. Garlic does smell like sulphur (and sulfur) because it contains same. That's where it derives its antiseptic properties.

What's missing this spot?

What's missing this slice from pizza?

s-m-a-l-l-(r)
beer-(ish)
g-a-r-l-i-c
o-l-i-v-e-r-s
a-t-c-h-k
a-l-r-h-o-m

Medical studies conducted in India show that 10 to 12 cloves of garlic eaten daily can raise good cholesterol and reduce bad cholesterol levels in the blood.

If you burn it while cooking it will turn bitter.

pest-free

Tea

This one is for bug-spray, not for biscuits.
To one liter of boiling water add: 3 tablespoons chopped garlic cloves
2 tablespoons grated soap. (rinse grater thoroughly afterwards!)
It will help your plants repel insects and fungal spores.
Cool to room temp before use.

Garlic helps bust up blood clots.

You can purchase it as:

Dried, single heads

Braided dry heads (decorative, too!)

Chopped in its own juice

Powder or granules; with or without salt

Garlic is a good friend around the globe, but best **not** planted near...
(but roses love him)

(Nothing personal - just bad chemistry.)

strawberries   cabbages   Peas or Beans

Be Sweet to Me ~ but not too sweet.

Sugar is sweet. How sweet are you? Most kids like the taste of sugar. A little something sweet can make you happy. Someone who really seems to crave sugary treats is said to have a "sweet tooth," but a tooth can't actually taste anything, and your teeth will greatly benefit from a brushing, following a sticky snack. It takes as little as fifteen minutes after sticking to your enamel for sugar to feed the acids that like to nibble on your teeth. You may smell a batch of cookies baking in the oven, but you can only perceive their sweetness on your tongue — which has about ten thousand taste buds! So when we say, "I want something yummy for my tummy," what we really want is something yummy for our taste buds. Besides that, many of those thousands of tastebuds would actually prefer something sour, salty or savory to a dose of sucrose (or maltose or lactose or ... read on).

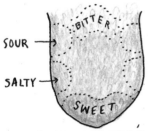

SOUR →
SALTY →
BITTER
SWEET

YOUR TONGUE'S SENSORS

SWEETNESS CAN GET OLD WITHOUT THE OCCASIONAL CONTRAST OF THE OTHER TASTE SENSATIONS.

Have you ever tried rock candy? It is made by crystals formed around a string dangled into a pot of boiling cane sugar, and possibly the sweetest thing I ever tasted (ugh...)

MANY MEDICINES ARE BITTER IN TASTE BECAUSE THEY ARE ALKA- LINE (high pH). Foods like zucchini can taste bitter. Cucumber peels are ultra ⌣.

SO SOUR YOUR TONGUE SHRIVELS? YOU JUST TASTED AN ACIDIC FOOD. (can super sour gummy worms be considered food??) Lots of fruits are sour before they ripen, and some remain sour forever!

SALTY FOODS MAKE YOU THIRSTY (it's osmosis at work) AND WE ALL CRAVE SOME SALT. JUST DON'T OVERDO IT. Even unsalted potato chips contain some natural sodium found in the potato.

Save your teeth. You will still need them when you are too old for Trick or Treat, even if you still enjoy a candy bar now and then. The smartest way to take your sugar is not by the spoonful, packet, cube or **confection** (does that last word sound like a blend of concoction and infection? It's just an old-fashioned word for a candy, cake or other "sweet").

I'M NOT A PINE AND I'M NOT AN APPLE, BUT I AM ONE OF THE SWEETEST THINGS AROUND!

The sugar inside a fruit got in there by way of an ancient, natural process and won't confuse your body the way manufactured, concentrated sugars can. When pineapples were introduced to Europe they started a craze!

Sugar and you.
A LOVE/HATE RELATIONSHIP

This is your brain on sugar, which is how your brain functions! Of course, the sugar your brain needs to power its busy workload must be converted into the form called glucose. Whatever we eat our bodies break down, through digestion, into fuel and waste. The fuel that gets carried through the bloodstream to all the hungry cells in our bodies is a converted sugar called glucose. Just as you must have protein, fiber and healthy fats, you couldn't live without glucose. The pancreas is a vital organ, releasing insulin to level out glucose tolerance. Overtaxing the pancreas through long-term sugar bingeing can lead to a condition called diabetes. Anyone born with that disease would tell you to appreciate all that your pancreas does for you, and go slow on sugar.

Sugar, is that you?
BETTER LIVING THROUGH CHEMISTRY

Numerous artificial sweeteners have been formulated in the lab, in the quest to develop sugar alternatives that don't cause tooth decay, weight gain and other health risks. Scientists set to work mimicking the nucleotide chains found in natural sugars. The resulting products tend to have names ending in "ate", "ine", "tol," "ame" and they all too frequently wind up in the news due to cancer warnings and recalls.

Goodnight, sweet prince.

We humans truly love to experiment on ourselves, don't we? The perfect sweeteners already exist, and have done for millennia. They are inside our fruits, which we should be eating more of every day. There is also honey, a gift from bees.

Sugar ~ you grew!
I COULD TELL YOU WERE SWEET FROM ACROSS THE STREET

There are plants we cultivate for their sugars. There is also a long history of calling plants sweet- "something" – typically for the often cloying (that means choke-y) fragrance they emit while in bloom. Many of these are best appreciated from a distance!

Sweet Alyssum
Sweet Bay
Sweet Bergamot
Sweet Bouvardia
Sweet Box
Sweet Briar
Sweet Cicely
Sweet Flag
Sweet Gale
Sweet Gum
Sweet Olive
Sweet Rocket
Sweet Sop
Sweet spire
Sweet Sultan
Sweet William
Sweet Woodruff

↑ SWEET BOX

So sweet of you, Nature!

Glucose, the sugar of life, glues us together, in a sense, but that's not what the 'glu' stands for. The 'ose' at the end can be found in the name of any naturally occurring sugar, as in

fructose: fruit sugar

lactose: milk sugar

ribose: the sugar in your DNA ~ deoxy-ribonucleic acid ~ the fuel for the 'brain' of every cell, the nucleus.

maltose: barley sugar

amylose: starch sugar

dextrose: corn sugar

sucrose: sugar sugar, (but not honey honey), derived from sugar cane, but found in most plants— which also enjoy a sweet carbohydrate at mealtime

Sugar cane, or Saccharum officinarum, is a tall tropical plant whose successful introduction from the Canary Islands to the Caribbean made life miserable for the native people forced into the back-breaking labor of plantation work while it made life ten times sweeter for plantation owners and anyone who could afford to eat it.

Sugar beets are too woody to eat, but they add vast, domestically-grown supplies of sugar to our food manufacture. You won't find it in a cute little squeeze bottle, but corn syrup— and cornstarch—turn up in thousands of food products – few of them as good as good ol' corn!

Dry dates from a date palm, and you can turn them into sweet date sugar.

Maple syrup is made from sap that drips into buckets from taps driven into maple tree trunks.

Time's Fun, When You're Having Flies.

Frog Heaven,
24/7

CHIGGER WARNING:
THE FOLLOWING CHAPTER IS CRAWLING
WITH CREEPY CRITTERS. SKIP THE
NEXT DOZEN PAGES. LOSE TWO POINTS.

Chapter Nine

Eco-Existence
Pests and Pals

HABITS OF (*habitating*) CREATURES

There is room for all of us, big and small. Not everyone likes to cooperate, and some of us tend to take a larger share, but toxic warfare unleashed upon the tiniest among us poisons the atmosphere for the rest of us. We are not the only creatures in the garden, and there are gentler ways to protect what we tend than "nuking" the cabbage worms with products whose labels read **WARNING!** and **DANGER!** If you visit your garden every day you can check on your plants and spot insect activity before it gets out of control. You can also learn to identify the critters you see crawling around. Often what you think is a pest is actually a friend, a hungry **beneficial**, who will munch on whoever is munching on your leaves. Remember that many birds feed on insects, and if we poison their food we risk making them sick, too.

Sometimes your garden will be invaded by a species that multiplies so quickly you will have to resort to spraying or sprinkling. On those occasions there are still less-toxic remedies, and some of the ingredients are probably right there in your kitchen (remember that garlic tea!).

I enjoy watching all the creatures in my garden ~ the birds who visit the feeders (and leave thank you droppings on my lawn chairs), the squirrels who chase eachother up and down the tree trunks. My trees are finally big enough to support squirrel nests, but the most exciting nest was a thimble-sized cup formed of lichen and spider silk, home to a tiny hummingbird and her even tinier chicks.

You have room for pests and pals in your garden.

Can you find room for them in your heart?

WHO'S THAT LADY?

She's none other than _Coccinella*_ !

Whether you prefer to call them LADYBUGS or LADYBIRD BEETLES, these small creatures are among the best garden friends you can find. Next to the bees, ladybugs are our favorite **beneficials** ~ insects doing good things in the garden. By the way, Lady is actually about this [🐞] size.

The classic ladybug, as depicted in art ~ including the rather alarming lady here ~ has a red-to orange outer wing (her "shell") with up to three spots. Some have no spots, or red spots on a black shell, or black spots on a yellow shell. They even come in brown with white spots. All are members of Team Hungry Ladybug. Beware impostors!

[Actual size: ⬎]
What are those weird, miniature alligators on the roses??

This is an APHID. [actual size: 🐜]
It is also known as a plant louse. When your kale leaves become infested with aphids it looks something like this 🟫 , which will be highly unappetizing to you, but will present a feast to Lady, who will make short work of them. Well, she herself won't be dining on aphids, but her babies will. How did those horrid plant lice show up so fast? A mature aphid has wings. It flies into your cabbage patch and proceeds to lay dozens of young ~ _live young_ ~ by-passing the egg and larval stages. Creepier still, those young can be born pregnant! Aphids also come in silver-grey and black. They are particularly attracted to birch trees ~ whose aphid-covered leaves will rain a mist of **frass** down on everything below ~ and to **nasturtium** plants. If you add some nasturtiums into your veggie garden plan, they will serve as aphid magnets, drawing the fiends away from your delicious salad ingredients.

Meet the aphids' nemesis, a LADYBUG LARVA. Some gardeners are unsurprisingly alarmed at their appearance, which barely resembles their familiar, adult beetle form. Once you have learned about the larva's astonishing aphid-devouring capacity ~ up to ten times her own body weight ~ you will have joined her fan club. Try to resist handling the larvae, however. They are easily injured; and they are known to bite in self-defense! If you are out weeding or pruning, look out for larvae and for eggs, so you don't end up sending these allies to the compost factory. Larvae pupating into beetles cling onto leaves, benches, fenceposts, etc. Do not disturb.

EGGS

* There are 150 species of Ladybird Beetle in the U.S. and six thousand known species in the entire world!

The "B" Team

They're BIG! They're BOLD! They're...

Beneficials

(Actually, they're not all so big, but they are very big helpers in the garden.)

but have you ever seen a PRAYING MANTIS? In hot climates he can get even bigger than this one, but at any size a mantis is a fascinating — and hungry ~ creature! Mantids (not mantises) belong to the same scientific order as grasshoppers, crickets, katydids, and cockroaches, but they are more favorably received among humans. They feed on crop-destroying insects and don't scurry under the kitchen cabinets when you turn on the lights.

PARASITIC WASPS are really about this big [ ] and resemble small, winged ants. While we tend not to appreciate the many industrious activities of ants [submit your complaint here:], these busy little wasps employ what looks like a stinger to insert their eggs inside aphid bodies. The young wasps hatch and eat their hosts out of house, home and existence.

WHEN YOU FIND A HOLLOWED-OUT APHID, THANK A FRIENDLY WASP.

You have already met LADYBIRD,

This is a CARABID GROUND BEETLE, which really grows to about this size. It looks somewhat threatening but it presents no danger to you.

Like the strong-jawed TIGER BEETLE, Carabids seek out harmful insects in leaf piles and other debris on the ground. Try not to step on them ~ they're not interested in eating you.

GREEN LACEWINGS are about [ ] in size, and cloaked in delicate, sparkly green wings. Lacewing larvae look a lot like those strange ladybug alligators, only they are yellow-green in color. Lacewings also have a thing for ~ and against ~ aphids, building small pits in the ground as aphid traps.

it's a
BUG-EAT-BUG WORLD

Beneficials are out there scarfing up and chowing down on the bugs that bug you and me and anyone else who is just trying to grow a few salad greens. Some of our insect pals get so voracious ~ especially while competing for vanishing aphids ~ that they occasionally resort to cannibalism. I wished to keep a couple of mantids as short-term pets one summer. Here is what happened.

The Ballad of Brownie (and Greenie)

They do seem to be studying us, too.

when Brownie first hatched out of the egg case, he was about this big.

when Betty gave him to me to take home he was this big. He shed his skin and

grew to about this size. I moved him to a bigger jar. He shed again, and ate Greenie.

At five or six weeks old he began to shed for the third time, but it went badly....

A bug-loving lady named Betty purchased a mantis egg case from the nursery. She planned to release most of the hatchling nymphs into her garden to eat the aphids. A few would be kept back, in a jar, as pets. I expressed an interest in them, so Betty promised to bring me a few, once they were big enough to separate. A few weeks later, she appeared with a mayonnaise jar containing a couple of twigs and some aphid-covered leaves. Only two of the four or five nymphs survived the first week. I moved them into a larger mason jar, enriching their environment with more branches and a dawning realization of how much work I'd made for myself, delivering them a daily, catered menu of living, moving prey. In an uncharacteristically lazy gesture, I dubbed the green mantis, "Greenie" and the larger, brown one, "Brownie." Like a molting snake, Brownie underwent his first shed, zipping off the suit of skin that he had outgrown. He successfully passed his second shed, but Greenie, grasping a branch in preparation for his own costume change, must have looked more delectable than the gnats and inch-worms I had laid out for lunch. At the end of the day, all I found of poor Greenie was a leg. Meanwhile, the ladybugs had done such a thorough job of despatching aphids I was trekking further down the alley in search of food for Brownie. Feeling that I must have been losing a measure of my sanity, I ventured to the pet store to pay money for some wingless fruit flies, a self-renewing food supply, as long as Brownie spared at least a couple of them so they could repro-duce. Sadly, it was a fruitless, wingless effort. Brownie lost his two middle legs while undergoing his third molt, a seemingly unsurviveable injury. I released him into one of my larger container gardens, where he spent his final hours. Rest in Peace, Brownie, and Greenie ~ whom you ate.

On the boards and in the boards - it's

The Worm's Turn

The casting call is out for this year's performance of the **Wonderful World of Worms.** The gardening season being brief, opening night will happen in about two weeks' time, allowing for rehearsals, set and costume design. This will be an off-off-Broadway production. Must we travel to the **Big Apple** to catch our segmented stars' moment in the spotlight? Perhaps it's time to dispel some wormy myths.

1. You have just bitten into a juicy, fresh-picked, un-sprayed apple. To your exaggerated, theatrical horror you discover a rude little green worm, chewing through the crispy center— equally horrified by your over re-acting (sheesh, what a ham!). Put your eyes back in your head— it can't harm you — even if only *half* of the little guy is still in the apple (pooey-poo). Guess what —he's not even a **worm.** That little green squirmle is actually a larva, like the Ladybird Alligator, who is merely portraying an alligator — kudos to the costume and make-up crew! Every stage larva — or, insect in its **larval stage**— is simply going through a phase, waiting to grow legs and wings, and be discovered for its hidden talent. Every **true worm,** on the other hand, will never quit its day job, tunneling, leg-less, through the soil and chewing, wingless, through debris. After that trouble-some green caterpillar drops out of your apple — provided he has kept his head — he will spin a cocoon and pupate into a moth or fly. Of course, some butterflies are beautiful ingenues, but the codling moth who has infiltrated your apple and the tent caterpillar who can strip an entire tree of its leaves are both bad actors, truly chewing up the scenery.

2. You lift up a flowerpot on your patio, to discover, writhing on the concrete, a dozen baby red earthworms, suddenly exposed to daylight. Do you drop the pot back on top of them and run away, screaming? A clever gardener might pick up the watering can or hose and gently wash the wormlets from the pavement into the lawn or nearby flowerbed. Earthworms not only like to be wet, they need to stay wet, or they'll shrivel up and die. That is why you will seldom see a worm basking in the sun like a caterpillar. You may see one making its way across the sidewalk after a downpour, but if it's stranded out there on dry cement, it probably was dropped by a distracted bird. (Perhaps the bird — about to enjoy its early breakfast — had caught the eye of a stalking cat and took off for a safer elevation.) If he's still alive and in one piece, perhaps you might help him make it to the grass. Don't squeeze him too hard, and applaud his performance as an

LITTLE HELP?

aerating, fertilizing, under-celebrated garden star. (Rescue is similarly called-for should you find a wriggling worm in a puddle. They are not good swimmers, and only work well in water as fish bait.)

Central casting: They may look interchangeable, but try to avoid type-casting them. They are literal gold-diggers ~ tireless agricultural helpers who contribute more work for less pay in aiding the development of healthy soil. While they tunnel through the damp ground, opening up space to aerate roots, earthworms are ingesting soil (eating dirt — don't try this at home). They pass the soil through their simple, tubular bodies, and what comes out the other end is a rich, organic fertilizer we call, **castings.**

A chorus line of earthworms, wiggling in unison, present an endless pageant of show-stopping talent. They can't sing like a cricket, but they can sure bust a move.

Other impostors and impersonators: The "Inch Worm" is actually the larva of a fly. It is also known as a leaf miner, due to its destructive habit of puncturing a leaf's surface and eating a winding trail between the outer membranes, turning the green tissue inside to a hollow, poo-strewn maze. You can keep this pest out of your spinach and chard by covering baby plants with a gauzy fabric called a "floating row cover," to keep the fly from laying its eggs on your tender crops.

A LEAF-MINER BAILING OUT, HIS WORK DONE.

"CABBAGE WORM" IS ALSO A MOTH LARVA

The "Meal Worm" is a grain-infesting moth or weevil larva. If you open up a box of breakfast cereal and a small moth flies out, chances are good that its pals are in there, too. Ditto for the buggies who float to the top of the bowl when you add milk...

OH O's now with chewy bits!

WORMS ATE MY HOMEWORK

The "Book Worm". You are the good version, who can't get enough of reading, but "paperworms" — larvae — have destroyed many an antique book and historical document!

it's
A BUG'S LIFE
(even if you're not a **bug** – per se...)

Perhaps it would be more accurate to call it a bug's **world**. They vastly outnumber us, they show no signs of leaving, and they stand to become a protein-packed, low fat menu staple. Let's meet – if not eat ~ "THE BUGS", and look at what they do.

Bug 'BAD' vs. Bug 'GOOD'

Bug 'BAD'

- Damage to crops
- Damage to homes and other wooden structures
- Stored grain contamination
- Venomous bites and stings
- Disease-carrying vectors
- Blinding swarms

Many insects feed on trash, helping to break it down faster. Some lay their eggs in animal cadavers to ensure a first meal for their creepy kids.

Bug 'GOOD'

Pollination

Food for amphibians, fish, birds (...us...)

Biological research

Useful commercial products, such as honey, wax, dyes, silk, shellac

Soil aeration

I repeat, pollination. We'd be in serious trouble without them!

All bugs are **insects**, but not all insects are **bugs**! In the realm of scientific classification, **true bugs** ~ I cannot lie ~ are just one small sub-classified branch of the insect **kingdom**. Well ~ technically ~ they are all part of the **animal kingdom**, further divided down through phylum, class, order, family, genus and species, just as we talked about with cats (in chapter two). The insect order **HEMIPTERA** is where bugs belong, and we wish some of them would simply **stay** there – especially the **stink bugs** and the **bed bugs**! (Others may have a soft spot for the colloquially snug, 'two bugs in a rug'.)

Hemipterids — members of the bug order — share in common the following identifying characteristics.

eeeeek!! a bug!!

Side-view of a bug's head (not a ghost running away, screaming).

←"beak" has a sucking mouth part (no chewing ~ yes piercing) which attaches near the bottom or back of head (not at top or front).

↑antenna mounted low (not up on the roof). antennae segmented.

thick wing base

front wing

back wing

A LEAF BUG.

There are too many species of true bugs to list here without bugging everyone unnecessarily, but I must make one important announcement: a Ladybug is not a bug, but a **beetle**. Ladybird beetles belong to the order COLEOPTERA. Coleopterids share a hard wing cover, lending that tell-tale crunch underfoot (not a suggestion!!!) and a carnauba wax shine. The beetle order (not John, Paul, George and Ringo) includes among its fascinating and varied members an array of amusing common names. In its ranks you will find the Snout beetle, Handsome fungus beetle, Pleasing fungus beetle, Boring beetle, Dung beetle and the Lightning bug (not a true bug!). Beetle "shells" come in complex patterns and attractive colors. Hobbyists —as well as scientists known as Entomologists— have been known to keep preserved display collections of Scarabs and their kin, much as has been a tradition among butterfly fanciers. Even the most "boring" of the beetles is worthy of a second look:

the metallic WOOD-BORING BEETLE. (It's not his dull personality ~ it's his occupation.)

and his cousin

the LOCUST BORER. (not a locust insect, but an insect that bores holes into Locust trees.)

Mouth parts, as mentioned above, are designed by nature to help devour plant parts — or bug parts— efficiently.

CHEWING: grasshopper jaws — toothless — chomp like our own do. Root weevils, slugs and caterpillars chew, but slugs use raspy "tongues".

SUCKING: robber fly pierces plants with a stylet— a needle-like straw.

SPONGING: house fly slurps whatever it finds with its bulbous proboscis.

and SIPHONING: moth — stranger than science fiction. (Remember, they are actually smaller!)

129

the BEE~ALL and END~ALL

Where would we be without the bee?
In a poorer state, indeed.
Working tirelessly for his colony,
Caring little for his own need.
One bee may travel twelve miles in an hour
Gathering nectar for honey,
Endlessly moving from flower to flower
And not for one penny of money.

A bee uses 22 different muscles to sting.

Honey bees can distinguish between sour, sweet, salty & bitter.

BEE FACTS

Largest: the bumble, at one inch long. Smallest: dwarf, at 3/8 inch.

A bee colony can have as many as eighty thousand workers.

Fossil bees trapped in amber lived as long as fifty million years ago.

Busy Bees

Apis mellifera, the HONEY BEE
The honey I make is the sweetest thing.
There'll be plenty for all, so don't make me sting!

Possibly our most important imported animal, Apis is not native to the U.S. The tireless work of this tiny creature feeds man and beast. Each honey bee colony — or hive — is populated by as many as one thousand bees, every one of them hatched from eggs laid by a single queen. Every bee in the colony has a job to do. Caring for the developing eggs and feeding the hatchlings is the constant occupation of the nurse bees. Worker bees make dozens of flights per day, between flowers and hive, transporting their harvested pollen. The bee's "knees" are used as saddlebags, where they collect the sticky, golden dust. Mid-morning is their favorite time to harvest. Carpenter bees construct the wax honeycombs, where the babies are developing and a supply of food is stored. The queen is waited upon like true royalty, and has no reason to leave her hive. Her only job is to lay more eggs. Beekeepers are humans who have, for centuries, learned how to do a diplomatic dance around bee-dom, gently removing golden honey for our use while leaving enough for the bees.

If you have not been initiated into the ranks of Bee Diplomat, you should do your best not to interfere with bee business. They are not interested in your comings and goings, but if your activity threatens their home, they come prepared to deliver a nasty sting. In this defensive maneuver the bee has sacrificed its own life. The stinger has a venom sack attached, so if it is visible in your skin, pluck it out A.S.A.P. Ice helps the pain subside, and a paste of baking soda will draw out the venom. You didn't mean it, and neither did the bee.

OUCH.

Bombus (over 250 species!), the BUMBLE BEE

What's yellow and black and fuzzy all over
And comes buzzing out when you run through the clover?

Bumblebees make their homes in the ground, often down abandoned mouse holes. One special feature — besides their cuddly appearance — is the fact that they will visit flowers in the rain, while honey bees wait out the weather inside the hive. The bumble bee queen lays all of the eggs and has a coterie of workers, but unlike the honey bee queen, she doesn't hold sway over a year-round, permanent hive. A new nest is built each spring, in which she will lay and tend her eggs, but she is also free to move about the garden, collecting some of her own pollen. She will stop laying eggs when the weather turns cold and pollen sources go dormant.

Megachile rotundata, the LEAF CUTTER BEE

Those holes in your leaves were not made by a punch.
I'm munching, but they're not my lunch.

LEAF CUTTER
CUPS, PACKED
INTO A HOLE

Leaf cutter bees cut perfect circles along leaf edges by chewing a 360-degree line. It is an amusing feat to observe, as they meticulously complete their precision rotation. They take the nibbled punch outs away to their nests, where each one is shaped into an individual cupped cell, ready to hold a leaf cutter egg.
They will return many times to the same plant, sometimes threatening to turn it into swiss cheese, but they rarely remove enough tissue to permanently stunt the plant. The munching will cease once their nests have been completed. They appear to choose soft leaves, which are available in abundance during the spring months.

Osmia lignaria, the ORCHARD MASON BEE

Tiny and quick, with black hairs on his back,
All he needs for a home is some mud and a crack.

GENTLE
MASON BEE,
RESTING ON
MY FINGER

A favorite of fruit growers, the Orchard mason bee is easy to introduce into the home garden. You can purchase their coccoons, which are made of rolled mud. When the adults hatch out, they will get to work pollinating. They will naturally roost inbetween the laps of old house siding, in un-filled nail holes and other small gaps, as they have done between my mailbox and the wall of the house or in the twinwall tubes of my greenhouse. You can also set up a purpose-built home for them ~ ready-made or D.I.Y. ~ of straws inside a coffee can or a wood block drilled with holes of a specified diameter. Orchard bees don't sting, so they are safe for people with allergies. They are also an important back-up for our declining honey bee populations.

Peculiar Bee-havior:

Bees "dance." Honey bees perform some elaborate choreography. Their curious bum-wiggling footwork is designed to direct their comrades to a newly scouted banquet spot or a relocated nest. It is bee sign language, and fascinating to watch.

Some bees are **nectar robbers**. Rather than wade through pollen-coated anthers at the tops of flowers, these bees prefer a shortcut. They tunnel directly into the flower's **nectary** by making a small hole at the blossom's base. This bypasses the pollen, and bean plants—often a favored victim of this daylight robbery—can suffer poor pod production as a result. You can see the telltale point of entry on some larger flowers, such as roses, camellias and peonies.

THIS WAY TO THE NECTAR BUFFET!

SMOKE MAKES THEM SLEEPY

SWEET BEE FARMS

A WOODEN BEE BOX

SNEAKY ENTRY

The Bee Industry:

Bees are well known for their industriousness, and are colloquial symbols of keeping busy and focused. There is also an entire industry that humans have built around bees. I mentioned beekeepers, and as honey bees are scientifically called **Apis**, a place where bees are kept is called an **apiary**. There you will find rows of man-made hives called bee boxes. Trays set into the boxes can be slid out—after the bees have been calmed by a bit of smoke—and their products can be harvested without harm to the bees or their keeper. Their most immediately thought-of output is **HONEY** – that long-treasured, healthful and natural sweetener. More than (!!!) 100 million pounds of honey are packaged in the U.S.A. each year. Before honey farms bottled their sticky, golden nectar they sold it in cut sections of honeycomb, slices of the actual hive, dripping with sweetness. Honey is an excellent energy food, packed with useful minerals. Infants have to wait a couple of years until their digestive systems can handle it, but after that they can enjoy it for a lifetime. Local honey that's been made from flowers growing close to home can help your body overcome seasonal allergies.

BEE KEEPER FASHION FUNDAMENTALS INCLUDE A BEE BONNET—A HAT WITH A NET TO PROTECT THE FACE. MOST SKIP THE GLOVES AND RISK SOME STINGS, FOR DEXTERITY.

QUEEN BEES ALSO MAKE PROPOLIS AND BEE POLLEN, WHICH HAVE ANTI-BIOTIC PROPERTIES

HUNNY

BAKLAVA

HALVAH

ROYAL JELLY

BEESWAX is exuded from living bee bodies, providing them with a strong and flexible hive construction and insulation material. Beekeepers spin honey out of the combs and then melt them in boiling water, to purify the wax. That wax goes into manufactured commodities, including candles, cosmetics, polishes, ointments, candy coatings, chewing gum, mustache wax, bikini wax, lip wax (balm) and wax lips. (Never seen wax lips? They used to come in cinnamon flavor, for about ten cents, in the 1960s, along with a six-pack of tiny wax bottles filled with syrupy "juice!")

WAX MELTS AND IS SKIMMED OFF THE SURFACE.

SHINY COATED GUM AND CANDY

BKBs

WAX LIPS (COATS YOUR TEETH)

WELCOME TO THE WEB-WIDE-WORLD

What's so wonderful about webs? Not much, if you are the fly who happens to get caught. They are works of simple, architectural genius, however, being spun from a seemingly endless reel of silk emanating from the weaver's own body, according to an ancient blueprint stored in its DNA. I'm not sure I could construct anything so efficient without a manual, and destroying a spider web as I make my way through the garden feels like a small act of vandalism. Luckily for the spider ~ who quickly nibbles the broken threads back into its body ~ the entire web-building process is impressively fast. That lunch-catching net will be back in place within twenty minutes. The cleverest spider will rebuild a bit higher, just above where its last web was ruined.

Orb-weavers construct the classic, circular spider web. They begin by dropping down from a high spot and sailing the breeze from the liquid thread they've attached up above. Once they have tacked the other end to a support, the scaf-folding is in place, and the fine details begin.

THE BASIC FRAMEWORK IS BUILT

START OF THE NET

SILLY STRING WITH A SERIOUS PURPOSE

"COME INTO MY PARLOR," SAID THE SPIDER TO THE FLY.

The liquid silk filaments dry and toughen in the air, lending them that telltale crackle ~ the one that lets you know you have just demolished a masterpiece, and had better check your hair for its displaced creator. You will often find the spider seated at the center of the spiral, waiting to be served its next meal. Should its dinner guest not arrive in a timely fashion, the spider may wander off for a good stretch, or to seek a drink of water. Not all species of spider execute such elaborate structures, and some simply nest in a hole in the ground. The most important thing **we** need to know is which of the species in our own environments — if any — might carry a dangerous venom. Most garden spiders might leave you with an itchy arm or leg, should they bite, but the venom of certain species is deadly!

THE WOLF SPIDER runs around chasing down its food. Females carry their egg sacs — filled with unborn young — wherever they go. The hatchlings, cling to their mothers back while she hunts.

A picnic-how thoughtful.

Why Grandma!

What a big family you have!

ARACHNIDA — that's the scientific class to which spiders belong ~ is made up of some 70 thousand species. All of them are creepy, by nature, but they are not asking us to like them. They are busy eating up mosquitoes and other pests. African and Native American folklore have tales of trickster spiders, members of our interconnected web.

TOAD in the HOLE

If you haven't seen these guys in nature, many of them live in the zoo. Pet stores carry some non-fishy aquatic and desert pals, too, best left in the desert. Collecting exotic pets can encourage poaching.

Keep in mind that reptiles and amphibians prefer their food to be alive and wiggling...

p.s.—
You wanna iguana? Start saving up — they are pretty pricey. A chameleon? I'd turn color.

"A toad in the hole is worth ten in the tub." It's true. Few wild creatures fare better in captivity, and that goes for the little frogs we brought home from camp. Suppose a froggie were to catch you and bring you home. How long would you survive in a cold, slimy pond, treated to a diet of flies and mosquitoes? It's not that unusual to come across **anurids** — frogs and toads — if you live anywhere near water. We had them in the brook behind the house in Illinois. There are plenty of other **amphibious** (at home on land or in water) and **reptilian** (cold-blooded four-leggeds) critters roaming people's back yards around the world. (Let's not forget the non-legged reptiles, the snakes — though I'm glad they're not in my garden!) I enjoyed the little lizards I met in Virginia, Florida and Texas. Here's a shout-out to my Little Sister, Esther, who braved her lizard phobia to scoop that wayward fella out of Mom's bath tub. Wish I'd been there!

Orders of magnitude, among the scaled and slithery:

ANURA: A toad is not a frog, but they have a lot in common.

WARTY SKIN, STUBBY LEGS

SMOOTH SKIN, SLENDER LEGS

Bufo, the toad — the *true* toad, that is. Other toads have these **generic** (genus) names: **Scaphiopus!** **Gastrophryne!!** **Rhinophrinus!!!**

RHINO., the MEXICAN BURROWING TOAD, BALLOONS WHEN ALARMED

Rana, the frog — the true frog ... there's also **Hypopachus!** **Syrrhophus!!** **Eleutherodactylus!!!** **Hylactophryne** (the barking frog)!!!! **Leptodactylus!!!!!** Acris, Pseudacris, and **Hyla** (the tree frog). (I rana outta exclamationa points.)

CAUDATA: the salamanders and newts.

AN EFT IS DEFT

A STRIKING RED EFT

These guys have such fabulous folk names as waterdog, siren, zigzag, hellbender, mudpuppy, cow knob, eft and mole. Salamanders are slippery, and must live in wet environments. Mole salamanders mainly dwell underground. All are active at night. Lungless salamanders ... have no lungs, and breathe through their skin.

A TENNESSEE CAVE SALAMANDER, THE BELLE OF THE BALL

TESTUDINAE: the turtles, tortoises and terrapins.

Here's an apt common name: "Stinkpot," the musk turtle. Its scientific name

NOBODY ASKS ME TO THE DANCE

is **Sternotherus odoratus**. There are so many kinds of shelled reptiles in this order — soft-shelled, hard-shelled, mud, box, painted, musk, gopher, snapping, sawback, map, cooter, slider, and sea — that they could fill their own chapter. To summarize, humans and turtles have long been at loggerheads. Turts and torts can make fun pets (we had them, before the Salmonella warning). Plastic spared countless tortoises whose shells might have become combs and decorative items. Now plastic fishing nets shorten their lives in the oceans. Turtle soup is not a hot menu item for most people I know, but turtle meat remains on the table in other parts of the world. The big 'T's live on every continent except Antarctica.

SQUAMATA: Lizards, geckos, Iguanid anoles, whiptails and skinks.

Ophiosorus, the glass lizard, has no legs but is not a snake. What they *do* have is a set of movable eyelids — a skink can blink — and external ear openings. Unlike supple snakes, they are stiff to the touch. (I have no hands-on experience.)

NO HISS-KISS KISS

UP TO BATS

Bats have had some bad press. They get blamed for carrying diseases. People are spooked by them because they fly around at Nighttime, in large swarms. They have oversized Ears – the better to hear you with, my dear! ~ and pointy little Teeth ~ the better to bite you with, my dear! ~ except that they are not very likely to bite You. Most species of bat feed on a diet of Insects, in impressive and unrivaled numbers, which they devour in mid-flight. True – there is such a thing as a Vampire Bat, but they don't hang out around here (although they do Hang out – sleeping upside down). Vampire Bats do not transform into men with Transylvanian accents. They do not suck Blood so much as they lap it up with a fluted tongue. (They do not say "Blah," unless you taste particularly bland.) You are more likely to be fed upon by a bed-bug than by a bat!

Myotis lucifugus is popularly known as the Little Brown Bat.

Bugs beware!

His body is only about four inches long but his wings spread over a foot. You may not see him, but he can certainly hear you!

Bats help keep the world's insect population in check. They are quite amazing little mammals, who fly by means of a thin membrane of skin stretched between their fingers and tail. They do not have feathers, like birds, but fur, like many of our cuddly pets do: I wouldn't recommend keeping one as a pet, but some people do put up houses for them, high up on a wall, for lack of a belfry. (Actually, as a welcome mat to a bat.)

Johnny Jumps Up

What is a **Weed**? Well, there are several answers to this question. A weed could be an uninvited plant that threatens to take over your tidy flowerbeds. It could also be something you planted ~ but later found objectionable ~ ugh! what a color! Ew! what a smell! ouch! what prickles! ~ and you want it to go away. Sometimes even a plant you still like will reproduce beyond your wildest dreams, becoming a nightmare by flourishing everywhere. A *volunteer* is any plant ~ even a seedling tree ~ that simply shows up in the garden by mysterious means. It may have arrived on the breeze, as a burr stuck to your sock or your dog's fur, or it may have been buried there "for later" by a visiting garden pest. **Pest**, or **pal**? It's a matter of perspective. Just as those precious Johnny Jump Up violets can become invasive, the cutest visiting critter can cause destruction. Every year I pull up the dozen or more hazelnut trees the squirrels planted ~ by stashing nuts for winter ~ and then forgot. Birds feast on wild blackberries and drop their seeds so prickly brambles can sprout. We can all be pests or pals, from time to time, so how about we try to ***link the Weed to the Pest who planted it***:

WORLD'S TINIEST VIOLA

Johnny,
Johnny, Johnny whoops,
Johnny whoops,
Johnny, Johnny
Johnny.

CORYLUS 'Я' US

4-ever...

OL' YELLER

the invincible taproot

come for the berries,
stay for the thorns
you're stuck on.

RAMBLIN'
BRAMBLE

Helpful
Schmelpful

Stealing
Starling

Flower
Fool

Nutty
Buddy

* FULL DISCLOSURE:
- I DRINK DANDELION ROOT TEA EVERY DAY.
- WILD BLACKBERRIES TASTE THE BEST.
- I FEED THE SQUIRRELS.
- STILL ON THE FENCE RE: STARLINGS...

* YOU CAN NEVER HAVE TOO MANY JOHNNY JUMP-UPS, REALLY.

BOYDZ IN DA 'HOOD

Birds are notorious graffiti artists. They're busy at work, decorating surfaces vertical, horizontal and everything in-between. They will tag buildings, cars, trash bins, statues, pavement, cyclists, pedestrians, picnic tables and other birds. They've simply gotta express themselves. Every Downtown has its pigeons. Near the Waterfront, the seagull gangs are out in full force. By the Lake, the geese make walking dicey. In City or sub-urb, the crow is king ~ bigger, louder, and always looking for a bite to eat. I can't complain about their creative deposits, as I have fallen into the thrall of the local **murder**. (That's not bloody gang war — a murder is what you call a collective of crows, or their related flock, much as you would have a **covey** of grouse.)

Crows are clever. A University of Washington study observed and documented the fascinating behavior of these well-adapted urban dwellers. Crows can recognize our individual faces and walking gaits. I returned to visit my old stomping grounds following a five month absence, and as soon as I stepped out of the car, a crow whose diet I had routinely subsidized with bits of dog biscuit began to trail me down the sidewalk. He landed, three or four times, just inches from my feet. I made sure to have a couple of crackers in hand for the return walk. At home, I began to toss my son's school lunch breadcrusts onto the carport roof. "Cracky"— king of the local **corvid** clan — would show up every morning for his hand-out. If I neglected to leave an offering he would perch atop the garden gate, waiting in the path to my car for his protection payment. Even cheese-flavored crackers — his favorite — were no guarantee against him or his compadres spelling out their initials all over the rooftop. Still, I didn't mind. He thanked me in his own corvid fashion, chanting a sequence of odd beeps and clicks. Once I watched him play fetch with a bottlecap, sliding it repeatedly down the roof and retrieving it from the raingutter. I assume he is gone now, but his descendants still visit this softie.

CRACKY WOULD BOW HIS HEAD UP AND DOWN, CLOSING HIS EYES WHILE SAYING, "BOP BOP."

Sparrow the HERO

Early one May morning, many cats ago, I was awakened by the sound of frantically screeching birds. Prepared to run out to the garden in pajamas to investigate ~ or intervene ~ I stopped short of the kitchen door. There, on the last step up from the basement lay a small, limp baby sparrow, still downy-feathered. It

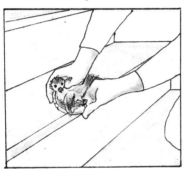

was barely moving, but intact. Was it out of screeches, with its tiny beak opening and closing silently? Could it have flown through the cat flap in the kitchen window? Where were its parents, and ~ furthermore ~ where were my mischievous cats? My felines are not permitted to range ~ roaming the neighborhood in search of songbird snacks. They have 24/7 access to a deluxe kennel on the deck, accessed via the window, yet not one of them was in sight.

I scooped the shocked fledgling into my hand and tucked it into a small carton, passing through the kitchen to the front room. There I encountered an unusual tableau: standing upright, still as statues, were four out of five cats, their eyes riveted upon the lowest level of my son's Hot Wheels® Super Parking Garage. A closer inspection revealed Papa Sparrow ~ as frozen as the cats ~ tucked behind the ramp to Level Two. I plucked him from that spot and

Mardi, Silvi and Zuni, out in their penthouse catio

set him in the box with his offspring. When I got out onto the deck, there was Mama Sparrow, screeching from the railing. Papa flew out from the carton, to calm her and escape me ~ likely in equal measure. I deposited the young one into the nest box they'd been using, out by the garage. They were back to feeding him within the hour, so it looked like his parents would not abandon him. Papa's heroic diversion tactics led to a successful rescue. My guess was that the baby had flown or dropped into the kennel and been snatched by one of my cats, as a toy. No one ever confessed.

Mardi, Boodle, Bina and Silvi check out Papa Sparrow's parking skills

SEASONAL EMPLOYMENT

Chapter Ten

Lore and More
Greeting Seasons

SEPT/MBER

TIM-BERRR!

That's the warning shout of the lumberjack. It means, "gang-way and look out below" to his fellow jacks and jills, because a tree has been cut and is about to fall. Trees do not always fall precisely where you expect them to, which is why tree felling is best left to the professionals.

Why do we cut down trees? There are many reasons — most of them logical — but we also have laws protecting some trees and government agencies enforcing those laws. The specimens we consider part of our legacy, like the ancient, giant redwoods and other heritage old-growth, might have been turned into somebody's barn, barracks or boat, if not for such protections. Timber management is crucial.

GOOD REASON #1: WOOD PRODUCTS: how many items that you touched yesterday began as trees? I can count: my hairbrush handle, trusty pencil (Sanislo Young Author Conference, circa 2002!), fir flooring, kitchen chair, drawing board, junk mail, important mail, cabinet door, house door, toilet paper...

#2: FOREST MANAGEMENT: flames jump from one tree to the next, rapidly creating the devastating wildfire spread we see each summer. By removing scrub and debris and thinning out trees, crews take preventive measures against future fires. Some fires are started by careless people, but most result from drought, winds and lightning strikes.

#3: LANDSCAPING: in both commercial and residential settings, we alter the environment to better suit our living and working arrangements. Trees are usually "in the way" of home building, roadways, railways, or potential farmland. My friends Connie and Carol milled the trees they cleared from their lot and used it as flooring in their new home. Sanislo Elementary school was cleverly designed to fit between the existing Douglas firs onsite, creating classrooms surrounded by trees.

#4: FUEL: since cave people discovered fire, wood has been harvested, chopped, stacked and burned. Woodfires are used for heating, cooking, baking pottery (raku), lighting, warming stones for saunas and sweat lodges. Wood burns cleaner than coal, and is renewable.

#5: CHRISTMAS: few things smell better than a fresh cut conifer. Do make sure, though, to source your holiday tree from a farm that practices sustainable culture. Never slip into the woods, park, Arboretum, Zoo or your neighbor's yard to cull a tree. Santa will not be impressed!

OCTUBER

What is a Tuber? It is a fleshy, starchy root, found underground, and used as a food storage pantry by the leafy, stalky, flowery parts of the plant attached to it above ground. Manioc (cassava/yuca) is a tuber we find useful. Most other tubers maintain a low profile through much of the year, catching our culinary attention in time for the autumn and winter holiday feasts. Tubers are versatile, and can be prepared in many ways. Perhaps you have tried Sweet Potato chips, Candied yams, Jerusalem Artichoke Stew? How do you feel about potatoes, potatoes, potatoes?

OCTUBERFEST

a contest in which two popular pies vie for first place at the table

They're both orange!

They're both mushy!

I yam what I yam.

FEELIN' LUCKY, PUNKIN?

'LEAST I'M NOT OUTTA MY GOURD!

I'll squash him

Sweet Potato Pie

A big hit, down South. Creamy, filling, and best right from the oven. The best-tasting vitamins you'll ever eat!

(I've a preference for pumpkin ~ I cannot lie ~ but in terms of nutrition, I'd say it's a tie!)

Pumpkin Pie

Alleged favorite with the Pilgrims. Sweet and spicy ~ great served warm or chilled. Plain, for breakfast. Add the whipped cream for dessert.

UNDERGROUND KITCHEN COMIX presents:
BACK to OUR ROOTS

How do? I'm your ancestor — an old-fashioned glass can. Today they call me a mason jar!

YES WE CAN!
Vacuum-sealed produce and preserves fed families over winter months.

Izzat so? I'm a modern, pull-top aluminum can, but as you can plainly see, I, too am ajar.

In the days before electric refrigeration — and in remote areas where the Ice Man cameth not — some people dug **root cellars**. Temperatures are cooler underground. Roots and tubers keep longer — and refrain from sprouting so fast — if kept cool.

WHO KNOWS WHAT LURKS IN THE DARKEST DEPTHS OF...

THE ROOT CELLAR?

Scary Sauerkraut from nineteen seventy-seven?

YOU do!

into every autumn some leaves must fall

just let go.

That is the Zen mantra of the deciduous tree in autumn. It is the natural way of things.

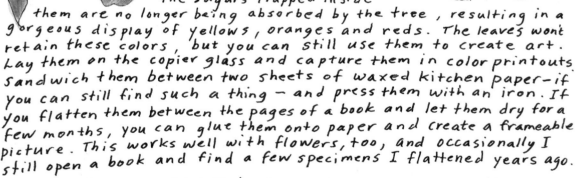

NYSSA "Tupelo"
QUERCUS "Oak"
ACER "Maple"
COTINUS "Smoke"

Let the leaves go. They have had their season. New ones will sprout along bare branches in the spring. For now, the sugars trapped inside them are no longer being absorbed by the tree, resulting in a gorgeous display of yellows, oranges and reds. The leaves won't retain these colors, but you can still use them to create art. Lay them on the copier glass and capture them in color printouts. Sandwich them between two sheets of waxed kitchen paper — if you can still find such a thing — and press them with an iron. If you flatten them between the pages of a book and let them dry for a few months, you can glue them onto paper and create a frameable picture. This works well with flowers, too, and occasionally I still open a book and find a few specimens I flattened years ago.

Autumn officially begins on the autumnal equinox, which has to do with the position of the sun in relation to the Earth's equator. The equator is an imaginary line, and the seasons are abstract units of time, but the voyage our planet takes around its life giving star (approximately 365 days of travel) is very real. We can adjust our wardrobes by putting on a sweater on an unusually chilly September day, but we can't fool the trees. They know when the seasons are changing, and they have to do their thing. Fall colors are at their most spectacular when temperature shifts are gradual. Some years, the winter chill arrives suddenly, surprising the trees. Their leaves will drop, mid-transformation, or simply fail to fall. There they hang, limp and brown, until the winds do their job. I always hope for a fabulous fall, as it is my favorite season.

CORNUS "Dawgwood"

An Octoberpuss's Garden
in the shade

Denali is an October cat — that is to say, she was born in October. As far as I can guess, based on the size she was when Connie found her. A hungry kitten — left out of the head count as the litter's home was being sold — Denali appeared, as Connie turned the key for the first time. Where had had she been eating? where, live now? Her mom's owners she hidden? what oh where, would she didn't want her...

Connie called me at work. "I know you just lost Mardi, and it's probably too soon..." But it was never too soon for me. "It's a tiny Siamese — a lilac point, I think." I'll take it, I said. "Do you have a name?" Denali, I answered, without missing a beat, because I'd already known that my next cat was going to be white and that its name would be Denali. Not after the Native name for Mt. McKinley, but after Gumby's friend Denali, a woolly mammoth who could drink water and spray ice cubes from his trunk. (Thank you, Art Clokey, for Gumby and friends.)

Denali is turning eighteen this fall. She has seen many pets come and go from our household. She was an ideal auntie to Soliban, Paloma, Mirabai and Ruthie Bader, when Simone — my second pregnant stray — had her litter in the catio. Denali is the only cat who gets to lounge in the garden — in the sun and in the shade — because she can't be troubled to jump the fence. She is deaf and somewhat senile, and her bird-catching days are over. She is in her golden autumn years, and now older than any other cat I've had.

KNOWVEMBER

November was once the ninth month of the calendar year. Earth's annual trip around the sun neatly breaks up into twelve months, based on the approximately thirty-day waxing and waning of our lovely moon — whom we call, "The Moon". The number 30 is not evenly divisible by 7, and our weeks are seven days long, but twelve perfectly matched months of 28 days each creates a messy leftover blob of 19 orphaned days. Because the mathematical mind craves perfection, holiday ritual is more reliably remembered when tied to a regular schedule, and certain self-important emperors needed months named after them, we arrived at the calendar familiar to most of the industrialized world.

1 January IT'S WINTER. LOOK OUT THE WINDOW AT THE BIRDS. SLEEP IN WHEN YOU CAN. READ BOOKS AND SEED CATALOGS.

4 April FOOLS! NO, THE TOMATO STARTS AREN'T IN YET, BUT WE HAVE SOME GERANIUMS YOU CAN PULL IN AT NIGHT! (STINKY.)

7 July WHAT?? NO HEATWAVE? DON'T WORRY- WE'LL HAVE ONE FOR SURE IN AUGUST. EVERYTHING IS GROWING!!!

10 October HERE COMES THE RAIN. LET'S STAY IN AND TRY TO COME UP WITH MORE ZUCCHINI RECIPES!

2 February A FEW DAYS OF SUN! GO TO THE LOCAL NURSERY AND ASK WHEN THE GERANIUMS WILL BE IN!

5 May HOORAY! SPRING IS HERE! THE RAIN HAS (MOSTLY) STOPPED AND YOU CAN PUT EVERYTHING OUTSIDE.

8 August UGHHH. IT'S SO HOT... FOR A WEEK! WHAT? THE HEATER CAME ON THIS A.M.? SHUT THE WINDOWS...

11 November REMEMBER HOW MUCH WE MOANED ABOUT THE HEATWAVE? SURE MISS THAT SUN...

3 March A WEEK OF SUN! ASK WHEN THE TOMATOES WILL BE IN!

6 June GO CRAZY IN THE GARDEN, BEFORE NEXT MONTH'S HEAT-WAVE DRIVES YOU INDOORS.

9 September AHH! THE TEMPS ARE FINALLY PERFECT! JUST IN TIME FOR SCHOOL.

12 December QUICK- RUN OUTSIDE!! THERE'S AN INCH OF SNOW! LET'S MAKE A SNOWMAN!!

bizarre Oasis floral foam
Ha-ha.
Feb. plugs in the greenhouse
Even the Basil
your sales clerk

Our 'Western' calendar of 365 days — except in Leap Years, when February gets a 29th day (to help balance out the argument between the moon and the sun) — is called the Gregorian calendar. Pope Gregory made some adjustments, back in 1580 or so, to the existing calendar, which had already undergone some serious remodeling by the Babylonians, Greeks and Romans. The first calendar adopted by the Roman Empire named 10 months, covering a 304-day long year. (What of the other 60? They ignored them.) The months were Martius, Aprilis, Maius, Junius, Quintilis (5th), Sextilis (6th), September (7th), October (8th), November (9th) and December (10th). This sloppy arrangement had to be tweaked every second year, or the seasons would seriously begin to slip out of place, and before long, 'winter' would be falling in 'Sextilis' (as it does in New Zealand, incidentally). By the time Julius became Caesar (emperor), things were in such disarray that it was decided the year needed to be a consistent 12 months in length. Januarius and Februarius had already been squeezed in to absorb those annoying extra 60 days, but the seasons were still out of whack. For one year — now corresponding to 46 B.C.E. and called, in its time, 'the year of confusion' — Julius declared that there would be 445 days! In return for this edict, the month known as Quintilis was renamed July, in his honor. Eventually Sextilis would be changed to August after Caesar Augustus. The Julian calendar was close to what we use today, but Gregory's leap year scheme perfected it.

Thanks to the regularity of the Gregorian calendar, Americans can plan to celebrate an annual Thanksgiving feast on the third Thursday of every November. It works out well, because as long as November always falls in fall (Autumn) there will be plenty of pumpkins for pumpkin pie, cranberries for cranberry sauce, yams, hams and turkeys. The numerical date will vary, of course, as T.G. Day is not one of the holidays pinned to a particular number, like Juneteenth or July 4th. Not much else is happening in November — apart from Election Day (the second Tuesday) — so we are not likely to forget to celebrate it.

THE BEST CRANBERRY SAUCE WAS MADE BY HELEN HABER, WITH WALNUT HALVES.

MY THANKSGIVING FAVORITE, THE MILK CHOCOLATE TURKEY — HOLLOW, BUT SATISFYING.

JUMP IN THE LEAVES

Help?

YARD WASTE

DON'T JUMP IN THE BIN

November in the garden is fairly uneventful. In many states, plants are already tucked under a blanket of snow. In Seattle, the municipal yard waste authority lets you set out extra bags for collection at no extra charge. November is still a good time to go out and prune, but any leaves you neglected to rake up by then are a heavy, sodden muck, as the notorious Rainy Season (not one of the official calendar four) is well underway. Those traditional four seasons are not arbitrary divisions, either. Their old-fashioned names reflect what is occurring, in terms of temperature, day-length or plant growth.

The closest thing to the rainy season is the Anglo-Saxon word winter, which means "wet season", but November is still in autumn — a form of the Latin word for "maturing". Spring is Anglo-Saxon for "rising," and summer traces back to the Sanskrit word for "season." (I guess summer was prime time in ancient India. Who doesn't cherish the sun?)

MEET THE PRESS

$\mathcal{F}$all is harvest time, and after all of the fruits of spring and summer's labors have been picked, plucked, scooped, snipped, raked and otherwise gathered, it's time to decide to do something with all of them. Not all harvests are equally bountiful, but between your own garden and those of your friends and neighbors, there's a good chance you will be faced with too much of some good thing or other. Not everyone **cans** — although they probably could, if they knew how. Some fruits store well in the freezer, while others can be sliced and dried in the oven or in a dehydrator. When September arrives, one thing there is usually too much of is the backyard apple. Those rare, perfect globes that have escaped infiltration by maggots and codling moths (those notorious worm impostors) will keep nicely for months in the fridge or root cellar. But don't despair, if you see a hole or two in the skin or a bit of brown, crumbly frass on the bottom end. Cut the fruit in half. Unless it is utterly beyond edibility (a larvae-poo-palooza), you can carve around the invaders and their trails and cook applesauce.

$\mathcal{O}$r — you can look for someone with a **cider press**, and discover the deliciousness of fresh apple cider. Mix, match and blend your varieties, and everyone gets to go home with the best juice, almost for free. You will need some clean, empty jugs or bottles with lids. Some communities — and nurseries — have annual cider press events.

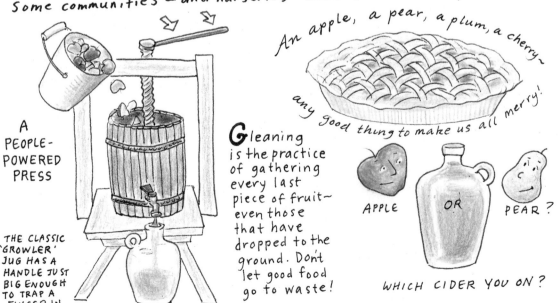

A PEOPLE-POWERED PRESS

THE CLASSIC 'GROWLER' JUG HAS A HANDLE JUST BIG ENOUGH TO TRAP A FINGER IN

$\mathcal{G}$leaning is the practice of gathering every last piece of fruit — even those that have dropped to the ground. Don't let good food go to waste!

An apple, a pear, a plum, a cherry — any good thing to make us all merry!

APPLE   OR   PEAR?

WHICH CIDER YOU ON?

Treecicles

When the world becomes a frozen treat.

Holiday on Ice! That is what you get when the rain freezes onto the utility wires with a coating heavy enough to knock out the power. The electrical service is out, and so is school, work, the heat ~ unless you have a fireplace or wood stove ~ and hot meals ~ unless you have a grill or hibachi. Hooray! No school! Let's run out and play ~ except, oops, no running ~ it's insanely icy out there! Ever wanted to hike on a glacier or skate on your street? Slap on the cramp-ons and slip on your skates ~ or save yourself the effort and simply slip on the sidewalk. It is perilous, but it's also incredibly pretty. Every branch and evergreen leaf is encased in transparent, glistening magic. Take some photos, if you can safely get out there. If you have a bird bath, thaw it with some hot water.

The most intricate ice I've ever seen accumulated on the branches in January of 2004. Snow is still a fairly rare occurrence in Seattle, and ice storms even more unusual. On that particular occasion each individual raindrop froze as it landed on the plants, cars and fence posts, giving every surface the texture of crystalline snakeskin. It was truly beautiful, and some compensation for the utter chill we abided within our unheated abode. Polar fleece, a dozen candle pots, lapcats, board games and take-out teriyaki carried us through. We knocked icicle 'pan pipes' from the rain gutters and bagged them in Zip-locs to keep the fridge frigid and the freezer frosty ~ and to keep the gutters in place!

Gertie's tree landed on her car ~ no damage!

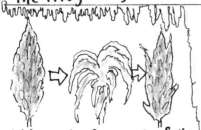

A blanket of snow is full of air and actually insulates the plants. Too much will bend or break branches, but most will bounce back after the white stuff melts.

FROZEN LEMONADE 25¢
no throwing, please.

When life gives you lemons, make lemonade. When life gives you snow, make snow cones. I miss Gina's Italian (frozen!) lemonade, but I do not miss freezing in Oak Park.

some broken branches will be future firewood.

Unless your wood pile was safely under cover, it would have been pretty challenging to find fuel for the wood stove, with all of that frozen stuff!

JUST WHAT IS THE MEANING

 OF 😊 🏃 💈 ☮ ♡ 🚦

THIS

We Humans are surrounded by symbols. We continually invent new icons to which we attach special meaning. Some symbols have a shared significance around the globe. Many, though, are limited to the cultures that agree upon their importance. Some have been imbued with such meaning that to deface, destroy or deploy them in the wrong context constitutes an act of insult or injury.

Some symbols lose all of their original power, over time, yet they continue to turn up — even if knowledge of their meaning has been re-interpreted completely. Can you name all of the icons up above?

Holidays are loaded with symbols — many of them quite ancient. One of the most recognizable winter holiday symbols is the Christmas tree, or *Tannenbaum*, and you might find its early origins surprising.

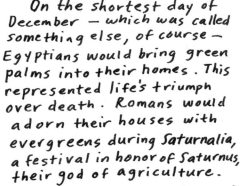

On the shortest day of December — which was called something else, of course — Egyptians would bring green palms into their homes. This represented life's triumph over death. Romans would adorn their houses with evergreens during *Saturnalia*, a festival in honor of *Saturnus*, their god of agriculture.

Druids decorated an oak tree with golden apples, and during the Middle Ages the Paradise tree was an evergreen festooned with red apples. This was done on December 24th, which marked the feast of Adam and Eve. The Christmas tree as we know it was introduced in the sixteenth century, in Strasbourg, Germany. Evergreen trees, decorated with colored paper, fruits and sweets were sold to villagers by old women, who would sit out in tree lots. The trees came from local forests. Early German immigrants and Hessians paid to fight in the American Revolutionary War,

TANNEN BAUMEN

brought along their tradition. In 1851, the first Christmas tree lot in the U.S. was set up, in New York. Trees were cut and hauled from the Catskill mountains to be sold in urban locales, where there were few wooded areas from which to source a Tannenbaum.

I grew up in Nassau County, N.Y., a moderate bike ride down the Hempstead Turnpike from Salisbury Park. Like Old Westbury Gardens — with the dew-soaked grass that ruined velvet shoes and the persnickety peacock — the grounds of Salisbury Park had once belonged to one individual. The owner had a stately home designed and constructed for his adult daughter. Eventually, the house became headquarters of the Historical Society, and the park itself was renamed after President Eisenhower — though it will always be Salisbury Park, to me. The first

timeless dust

fir? corn? cranberry?

floor — or at least what had once been the kitchen, living room or parlour — was open to the public. Next to the fireplace, year-round, stood a large, artificial conifer, strung with garlands of popcorn (real?) and cranberries (dried?). Therefore, when we arrived on our bikes, it was Christmas in July — or May, June, August... I think there were also lit candles decorating the tree, but those must have been electric, surely.

There are plenty of other plants with ancient symbolic meanings, related to the festivals and rites of various cultures. The *cornucopia*

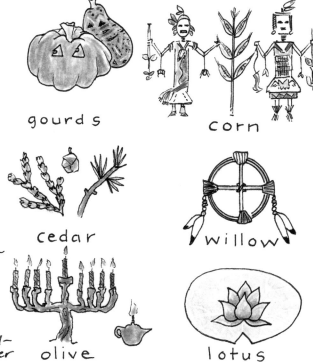

gourds

corn

HORN OF PLENTY

overflows with the bounty of a successful harvest. Many festivals acknowledge the gift of food produced by our fertile planet. Other holidays — holy days — utilize plants that represent spirits. Halloween evolved to be about candy, costumes, frights and...candy, but it was originally a more somber occasion — more hallowed — an evening and day to remember the souls of the dead — particularly dead saints — at least since the 700's.

cedar

willow

olive

lotus